WENDY BATTIN

ON THE LIFE & WORK OF AN AMERICAN MASTER

ISBN: 978-1-7344356-0-3

Published by Unsung Masters Series in collaboration with *Gulf
Coast*, *Copper Nickel*, and *Pleiades*.

Department of English	Department of English
University of Central Missouri	University of Houston
Warrensburg, Missouri 64093	Houston, Texas 77204

**Produced at The University of Houston Department of English
with support from the Nancy Luton Fund**

Distributed by Small Press Distribution (SPD) and to subscribers
of *Pleiades: Literature in Context* and *Gulf Coast: A Journal of
Literature and Fine Arts*.

Series, cover, and interior design by Martin Rock.
Cover photograph courtesy of Charles Hartman (Kalyves, Crete;
Wendy's 53rd birthday).

2 4 6 8 9 7 5 3 1
First Printing, 2020

The Unsung Masters Series brings the work of great, out-of-print,
little-known writers to new readers. Each volume in the Series
includes a large selection of the author's original writing, as well as
essays on the writer, interviews with people who knew the writer,
photographs, and ephemera. The curators of the Unsung Masters
Series are always interested in suggestions for future volumes.

Invaluable financial support for this project has been provided by
the National Endowment for the Arts, the Cynthia Woods Mitchell
Center for the Arts, and the Missouri Arts Council, a state agency.
Our immense gratitude goes to these organizations.

WENDY BATTIN

ON THE LIFE & WORK OF AN AMERICAN MASTER

Edited by Charles Hartman, Martha Collins,
Pamela Alexander, and Matthew Krajniak

THE UNSUNG MASTERS SERIES

gulf coast + COPPERNICKEL + PLEIADES
A JOURNAL OF LITERATURE AND FINE ARTS

CONTENTS

ESSAYS

INTRODUCTION

Charles Hartman

Wendy Battin was born on May 27, 1953, in Wilmington, Delaware, and died on December 21, 2015, in Mystic, Connecticut. Her great-grandparents were all Irish immigrants. Her poems are rarely directly autobiographical (it is remarkable how few of her poems say "I"), but in "The Telling"—a poem in intricate antiphony with the other poems in "The Women on the Ward"—she reconstructs the point of view of her mother. This is as close as she came in print to saying how she felt as a late and unexpected child, who early became eager to leave Wilmington. Though the family supported her desire to go to college (before marriage her mother had been a journalist), it was Delaware they had in mind; instead, she found her way to Cornell. From Julie Kane, her close friend and fellow poet, we have a warm account, reprinted here, of the undergraduate stage of Wendy's poetic career. She went on to the MFA program at the University of Arizona, but after a year left for the first of two Fellowships at the Fine Arts Work Center in Provincetown, where she drove dune-buggy tours (her license is dated May 10, 1977) and worked as an assistant to the artist Myron Stout.

I met Wendy in 1979 or 1980 when I was a junior faculty member at the University of Washington, and sat on her MA committee in 1981. She had been invited to apply by William Matthews, who was brought to UW from Cornell to run the Creative Writing Program. In an elegiac essay in the online journal *Waxwing* ("While I Was Sleeping"), Marcia Aldrich vividly remembers Wendy's presence in the UW workshops from the perspective of an awed fellow student. Later, in a letter for her professional dossier, Matthews would call Wendy "the best poetry writing student in the five years I taught there," and add that "the only poetry student I have taught in fifteen years who is comparable to Ms. Battin is Jorie Graham."

People who knew her early work felt affirmed rather than surprised when Wendy won the Discovery/*The Nation* Award in 1982. In 1984 her first book, *In the Solar Wind*, appeared in the National Poetry Series. In this series, inaugurated just a few years earlier, five books of poems are selected annually by prominent poets, Matthews in this case, and published by national presses. *Solar Wind* went to Doubleday. Unfortunately, this was when the Reagan Administration was cracking down on publishers' taxes. In earlier times a press would print a couple of thousand copies of a book of poems and count on occasional sales for decades—a system that depended on publishers maintaining a stock of their backlist. But after a 1979 Supreme Court ruling (*Thor Power Tool Company v. Commissioner of Internal Revenue*), the IRS changed its rules for business deductions in a way that made slow-moving inventory—including almost all poetry—more expensive to keep. In 1985 Wendy learned that a year after publication the remaining copies of her book would be pulped. She could buy copies at the author's discount, but she was living on writing residencies, and was able to afford only a small number of copies of *In the Solar Wind*.

After graduate school, the most obvious profession for her was teaching poetry. She did stints as a Lecturer at Suffolk and Boston Universities, and as an Assistant Professor for a year at Syracuse University. In 1992-95 she taught as Visiting Poet at Smith College, and later as Visiting Poet in Residence at Connecticut College and at MIT. She was a demanding teacher and sometimes a difficult one; many people expect a woman teaching poetry to be motherly, and though her relation to good students was supportive and illuminating, she was not motherly.

Another obstacle was that she had the wrong kind of degree: at the time, the University of Washington awarded writers an MA, not the MFA that was emerging as the "terminal degree" for poetry professorships.

The way around this quandary was to publish one's way into prominence, and that is what Wendy set out to do in the decade following her first book. She wrote slowly, however—though no more slowly than, say, Elizabeth Bishop—and it was not until 1997 that she finished assembling her second book, *Little Apocalypse.* This too won an award, the Richard Snyder Memorial Publication Prize from Ashland Poetry Press. Amazon lists the book as "temporarily out of stock."

Wendy was anything but a discursive poet, a fact connected with how little she liked writing prose. As she would say later in a Facebook post (November 11, 2014) when someone requested an essay from her, "I've always been a dichtung = condensare sort. Relaxing into prose, especially exposition, has always been a challenge." Her one published essay, reprinted here, is almost as condensed in its expression as we expect a poem to be. Her language-mind worked in vivid flashes—this was as evident in her conversation as on paper; she was a poet of what Ezra Pound called "piths and gists." A dossier letter from A. R. Ammons speaks of her "anguishing and powerful compressions of thought and phrase." Even in drafts and notes that never developed into anything larger, lines stand out everywhere as though they were trying out being whole poems: "There is no comfort for / a body out of love with itself"; "Canada geese stitching the water with their bills, to drink (like sewing machines)." In revision, she would have integrated that final simile more tightly into the sentence, probably as a metaphor.

Wallace Stevens's "Adagia" was a model some readers might refer to, its title taken from Erasmus's collection of Classical proverbs or adages. The Modernism that lay behind our generation's work was founded on the discovery that fragments, juxtaposed without explicit connective tissue, *were* the essential poetry. As Stephen Tapscott notes in his essay "Sequence and Dailiness" (included here), this is how Wendy's larger poems are almost always built. "Sense, Sensed" exemplifies how a poem can be assembled out of single gestures and images. After 1997, this act of assembly became even more visible; her "Four Poems" is such a construction. Occasionally the constructing might even be done by someone else; James Cervantes, editing an issue of *Porch*, proposed the group of her short poems that became "Elementals."

Cervantes was working from pieces that Wendy had posted on Facebook. At around the same time that *Little Apocalypse* was being published, the Internet began to be a venue more welcoming to a poetry of glints and gleams than print poetry magazines had ever been. Wendy was an early and active pioneer, first in listserv poetry groups like CREWRT, later on Facebook. This was also the time when she founded the Contemporary American Poetry Archive, an online repository for books that had gone out of print. (It still exists, vestigially, at capa.conncoll.edu, though the advent of Web searches has made it less necessary.)

Her books were not very often reviewed, and some reviewers expressed a peculiar kind of bafflement:

> Battin is highly interested in science. So much so her
> book is full of words like "drosophila," "diatom," "rotifer,"
> "bioluminescent," "echolocation," "stelazine," "coelacanth,"
> "anamnesis," "synchrotron," "sorus," "quarks"—words that stop
> this reader short. (Robert Phillips in *The Houston Chronicle*)

Wendy recalled an argument with another young poet who complained about her insistence on words like "larch" and "maple": "Why don't you just say 'tree'?" The right use of words, and the search for the most precise term, came along with her version of the Modernist heritage; her science and her Imagism were hardly distinguishable. Fortunately, other readers recognized this.

An unsigned notice in *Publishers Weekly* (September 21, 1984) appreciated that the work is "hard-edged and unsentimental, spare and deadly accurate, demanding of a close attention that is invariably rewarded." Pamela Alexander, whose review of *Little Apocalypse* is reprinted here, in a separate blurb called the poems "the waking dreams of a physicist: elegant, pure, accurate as light." Similarly, Janet Holmes (in *Crania*, Winter 1998) compared the poems to the photo on the book's cover: an x-ray of fingers holding the two-inch skull of an Eoraptor. Colin Morton observed that

> a Wendy Battin poem is continually transforming itself, permitting the reader to surf along on a wave of reference. This requires a trust that there's a steadying, [centripetal] force to all this whirl of thoughts. In large part, this trust is won through the rhythm, the sureness of craft, the poet's good ear. (Poetics. ca #1, n.d.)

Years earlier, J. D. McClatchy had included *In the Solar Wind* in a group review in *The Hudson Review* (Spring 1985): "She can be a bold but is never a capricious poet; she moves freely among startling associations and levels of imagery." He went on to say that "she writes with an austere elegance not unlike Charles Wright's or even some of Sylvia Plath," and hoped she would not cease "her fierce lyrical assault on the high places."

If the search for accuracy of meaning is one side of Wendy Battin's distinctive poetic language, the other side is her delectation of sound. She had little taste for conventional forms (though she wrote a few sonnets, Sapphics, and so on), but her poems are full of internal rhymes that link one line, not with the end of another, but with the middle of one earlier or later, making a tissue for which the inevitable analogy is weaving. Even if such plays of sound elude a reader's notice, they produce effects of musical unity all the stronger for being subliminal. Like

Pound—and like her other poetic true love, W. B. Yeats—she felt poetry as essentially music, and music as essentially dance. She was a gymnast early in life and a yoga teacher later, and all her life she loved to dance, which she did with a mix of abandon and precision that tended to make people on the floor gape. Once when I was grumbling about not knowing what my poems were *for*, she finally responded, "Well, I write poems to get people high."

Wendy and I re-met at The MacDowell Colony in 1992, and married in 1996. I was teaching at Connecticut College, and in 1997 was invited to shepherd a dozen students on a Study Away Teach Away program. I asked Wendy whether she could go without Internet for a semester. (She was already a denizen of the electronic world that had not yet reliably occupied the farther reaches of Europe.) Why? For a semester in Greece. "I could go without dinner."

A high point of that Fall was the series of archaeological field trips led eloquently and vigorously by Steve Diamant of College Year in Athens. One took us to Delphi, the ancient navel of the world, an epitome of all the Greek places we had both read about all our lives but never seen. About three days before that trip, on the way to dinner Wendy stepped off an Athenian curb and broke her ankle (for the third time in her life). A photograph shows her climbing the Hill of the Muses on crutches; unseen, a band of students cheers her on.

That year, 1997, her second book was about to come out. Of course she was at work on a third. Though it was never finished, at some point it took on the evocative title *Far Good*. In one note she calls it "the Greek book." Over more than a decade (we separated in 2009) we returned to Greece almost half a dozen times, living on Aegina for much of 1999, team-teaching at CYA for a semester in 2002, spending April and May of 2006 on Crete at the mouth of Souda Bay.

This volume begins with selections from Wendy Battin's two published books, *In the Solar Wind* and *Little Apocalypse*. The following sections collect material from the period after *Little Apocalypse,* some of it gleaned from notes and papers that—despite her fears, as reported in James Cervantes' essay—I gathered after her death. First come excerpts from the computer file containing *Far Good,* which seems not so much a manuscript as a running compendium of what that book might eventually include. Then we collect 16 finished poems from magazines, notebooks, and letters. The last section is a gathering of posts from Facebook; in that semi-public space, she did most of the work of her last years.

After the poems we reprint her one published essay, "Subterranean Maps: A Poet's Cartography," solicited by Sharon Bryan for the anthology *Where We Stand: Women Poets on Literary Tradition.* The next section, Early Poems, selects finished poems from before *In the Solar Wind,* including some work from the Cornell period. Most of this material was preserved or retrieved, with eloquently exceptional diligence, by Julie Kane.

After the early poems we present a brief Gallery of photos and images. There follow several critical examinations of Wendy's work. Besides Pamela Alexander's review, we have solicited essays from six other writers. Some knew her well, and it is natural that Julie Kane, James Cervantes, and Alfred Corn describe aspects of the poet's life. But she herself was "shaken" to realize "for the nth time that the life I have is the life I've written down" (Facebook, April 12, 2011); and a few months later, "Nothing matters more than the poems." Sharon Bryan's essay shows Wendy as she would have best appreciated, by unpacking one poem ("At the Synchrotron Lab") so that we can see a reader working to track the poet's language as attentively as the poet did. A different perspective is adumbrated by the set of annotations offered by John Gordon, a scholar of Joyce and others, who finds in Wendy's poems some of the dense allusiveness of High Modernism. Stephen Tapscott's essay, as already mentioned, explains the crucial role of the sequence in Wendy's work.

Finally, Notes and Drafts contains scanned images of a few of the papers found after Wendy's death. Some are handwritten fragments, giving the flavor of her lifelong work in notebooks. Others are printed pages (some quite early, judging by the typeface) that exemplify her habitual editing. The section includes early drafts of "The Restorer"—under its first title, "Dionysus and the Tiger," before she learned that the cat in the ancient image is taken to be a lynx—as well as "Mondrian's Forest" and "Letters from Three Women." The section concludes with the final page of *Far Good*, which illustrates the intriguing, unfinished quality of that book-in-the-making.

Besides photographs, the Gallery preceding the critical essays reproduces a small selection from the deck of Tarot cards Wendy made sometime in the 1980s: collages that allude, tangentially and wittily, to the standard Tarot deck, of which she owned a dozen sets. The Magician, for instance, features a CT scan of a brain, with a writing hand floating in nearby space. At some point Wendy worked—like Kepler and Galileo—as an astrologer, and enjoyed how this would have disconcerted Carl Sagan, whose astronomy courses she took at Cornell. She was certified as a Practitioner of Neuro Linguistic Programming; on a medical questionnaire she declared herself Buddhist. Her Catholic upbringing was far behind her from very early, though she fondly recalled the singing and the Latin. In a sense that I believe she would have embraced, everything she wrote was religious—though like so much else about her, this sense was at a sharp angle to the conventional. In the review mentioned earlier, J. D. McClatchy saw this center of gravity in her first book:

> She doesn't look to nature *for* metaphors; she looks to it *as* metaphor. I would say she has a deeply religious imagination, if that adjective weren't now suspect; let me say, instead, that she is, at her best, a quintessentially American poet. She has her eye on origins and ends.

SELECTED POEMS

FROM *IN THE SOLAR WIND*

Christine Falls on the Road to Paradise

Remember how sunlight drills
its own road through a cloud?
So that through the sky
there is a tunnel of sky.

Water falls from the sun-struck
edge of the glacier. It has no
bones, it has no intentions.
The sheer air cannot divert it.

The masses of granite and greenstone
cannot reach it. Only the simple
force on the supple
body of water moves it

down to the flower fields
of Paradise: farewell-to-
spring, larkspur, shooting
star, on the summer slopes,

stonecrop, higher and pale,
mountain misery, whose five
white petals splay in a wheel
like Da Vinci's man.

Is he rolling somewhere,
dizzy but perfected—
into the fireweed,
into the monkey-flowers?

Or to Christine, who died here
or was born,
or only remembered by someone
making a map.

She has left
her name to a pillar
of water, her monument
stubbornly forgetful.

—*Paradise Lodge, Mt. Rainer*

Astral Projection

I.

Each night my body leaves me, walks
to the brink of a city she imagines is yours,
though I tell her it's my place to wander, hers
to sink like an anchor through sleep.
I find her counting the lights that swim
below her, in the valley,
where thousands flip switches,
stroke gray cats. I cannot call her back.
And when she returns in the morning, stretches
out of her wake, I sense again
she has not found you.
It is not the old law of exile—just
the city rebuilding its walls,
this time to exclude her.

II.

To overlook the city at night
is to look at the sky: at points of light:
to look with the same fear of falling.
And each constellation a theory: connect the dots.
Out of this problem a building arises,
its random lights floating in the harbor,
its tenants peering into the world
like the drowned at a porthole,
their long hair streaming.
In the city the sky
rolls in and out like a tide,

on some nights remembered as it drains
away, on others
brimming among the rooftops as if they were piers.

III.

Only then do we know we've forgotten—mistaken
the electric lights in the park, each
a sufficient moon in its firmament
of leaves.
The trees glow as only the sky
holding the moon once glowed,
their lives uncovered like the heads of mourners.
But that is how grief in the city burns,
in commons where fear of the woods
is gone, where only the people harbor
death in the cultured forest;
where we are the ocean, the ground,
the sky and all our weather:
why we gathered here, and why we stay.

Billy Goat and the Tree of Life

after a statue found at Ur

What the Chaldeans saw
that set their hammers
against the original

gold is behind us. A goat
we assume is a god, because he stands
on two legs, as we do,

towers like a tree
against a tree. His forked trunk
grows, as we do, out of two roots.

But the tree rises as only itself
from the ground. And so we have
composition, the tripod

on which a lens can be mounted
to stabilize vision.
God the goat raises

his hooves in the branches. The tree
branches, branches as far as
the valence of metal allows.

They saw this perhaps
watching the goats
that went among them on

four legs, even in the city—
the city, their latest idea,
like an upstanding

goat, that stumbled
forward on language and
barter, always out of step.

The weight passed from my
hand to yours might have been
a word that you'd carry

the length of the clay-banked
channels we would call streets,
while the goats

wandered everywhere feeding
on everything,
asking what nothing was worth.

The Lives We Invite to Flower Among Us

*For just as that wild animal, if it shall have escaped and thus
recovered its natural liberty, is no longer the property of its
captor, so also the sea may recover its possession of the shore.*
—Hugo Grotius

Just as that wild animal, the sea,
is never in our midst, is constantly
our border, so also
a leopard, even in a zoo,
escapes us. He prowls
all our city's avenues, pacing
cage corner to corner, even
when we are most vigilant.

Set him free on the beach.
A body in a halo of senses,
he moves on the sand like water. The highest
wave casts down the shore like a spotted cat.
Nothing, our oldest lesson save one,
nothing is harder than water. The cat
on flat beach, the cat with no tree,
no ledge, as if caged,
cannot contain himself.

So also the thought containing the cat,
set in motion in a woman's
mind, a word
in a halo of sense. She makes
the leopard dark avenues
into the city of men, and then
she makes the seventh wave,

ending in foam just short
of the body poured out on the sand.
But even when she is
most circumspect, her mind

cannot contain itself, as a vase
may hold a flower but may not hold
itself. She loses the word
that stokes her into sense, that moving
cage and comfort.
The cat escapes
into the oldest lesson: no thing
is more yielding than water.

The woman rests
her mind in her body
in a halo of sense,
as if she were the sea,
and continent.

Letters from Three Women

We are moving from state to state,
as they say of excited electrons, or

of water when it freezes
and sublimes,

or the mind when it enters a drug
like an airplane.

When the letters bloom out of their envelopes
I think it must be spring,
remembering winter and the mailbox empty.
The pages collect on my desk, interleaved
like hands in a public oath. What
are we swearing to?

One has married her solitude,
wants a divorce.

One imagines that she
has not been understood.

One imagines she has.

The snapshot taken
through a fingerprinted lens records
identity and place: the smudge

floats in the doorway, a halo
whose saint has walked out.

One morning I watched from that beach
while a house rounded Long Point into the harbor.
Pennants, strung from the cupola
down to the barge, snaked in the wind and shot
the gulls through with panic.
The windows and doors had been boarded shut,
as if the house would founder if it woke.

You know me. I thought,
This is history: a house drifting sullenly
over the ocean.
Just look at the baggage we carry.

It docked at Macara's wharf for months,
waiting for cranes from New Bedford to lift it
bodily, as we all wait

in our rented rooms, or when
there's money, in apartments.
Today I receive you all in my room,
which dangles over traffic. The last one
huddled on a different city's ground,
under the weight of those
families I heard in the night,
like Hansel in the oven, listening.

I hear, for example, that lessons learned
drunk are best remembered drunk,
that the mind
knows this on the ocean and something

else at the kitchen table over coffee;
and think
especially of the humpbacks, who pass
their songs from ocean to ocean in
intricate barter.
                    Some days
I read you between the mailbox and my door,
the way we've eaten whole meals cooking them.
Is the ocean just a mind with a tune
running through it? The sun here

travels into an ocean
so monstrous we call it
peaceful, adrift on the land.

Cassandra

To speak at all I must pose
on the highest step, and squander
a week's ration of breath.

Bird squawk. Wind wash. You hear
what I say is abundantly
air, more rare

in space than the matter
with us, and the state.
The city rolls over the earth

like fog, without landing like fog
in beads on the grass first morning.
We tried mourning our own

passage into still life
because we had learned the word:
to mourn: the warm

pressing together of lips at its
beginning, and the tolling
of *our* in our throats on its way

to denial, *N*.
Who imagined the truth
was separate from its unfolding?

I've seen a ring around the moon,
as perfect as Euclid
and just that empty.

It held a huge dead world, cold light—
and the god who wanted my body
has taken my tongue.

The ring.
The moon nested there
threatens to hatch.

Lullaby

The woman in the next apartment trailed
home with a lover last night: soundtrack of keys

and voices in the hall, and through the wall
later the universal male moan, swinging

open the gate in the throat. What goes unheard
is seduction, and I thought of you

again, your body rangy among the voltmeters
and consoles. How accurate our backs are, turned,

triangulating the distance between those most
foreign objects, each other. This is a state

the priests called *immanence*, more blessèd
in the Godhead's privacy than here, in this

room of manifest tables. And this is in praise
of simple lust: the bodies pray themselves into

encompassing light. The brain thinks *not now,
not then*, but the bodies

think as computers think,
when the current runs through them.

Persephone Returns to Hades

This is no forced retirement; my job
carries me all summer to
the adits of abandoned mines.
You ask me how many ways there are
of slipping into the earth.
There's always a new route.

Like this: I wade
into the rain.
Like this: I take the subway.
I call it a career, as one careers
down a slope on skis.
          Forgive me. These meetings
are awkward as courtship.

The truth: I've come
through my mirror,
as always. I turned and saw
everything reversed, the leaves
on the brown tree growing
greener through the window.
I peered in and thought,
*This is a room I remember being
a woman in.*

This is the way I held my head.
And so I spend my winter
here, in your arms, watching
for skylights, chimneys,
the way out.

The Lighthouse Has No Keeper

I thought, tonight off Land's End nothing clicks.
The Bay is the same old kettle of fish,
geologically speaking.
A buoy rocks
under a cormorant, ringing
position.
        The black
fish-eater hangs its ragged
wings to dry, *spread-eagle* though
an eagle's wings spread out like entire
kites, unlike the kites on broken
frames the voracious
ancient cormorant angles out.
The snake-necked black
bird in the dark appears
only one second out of every thirty,
when the lighthouse sweeps it.
Its shape
splays like the fossil half-bird,
Archaeopteryx pressed in rock,
a feathered lizard with a toothy grin.

The lighthouse has no keeper, has
a clock of gears the mechanic
visits monthly. And
in fact the lighthouse clicks,
somewhere in its shell, behind
its diamond eye.

I am mistaken.
Somewhere in the Bay a dolphin
clicks. Its word in the water
is 31 meters long, a long word
uttered quickly.
I think the lighthouse has no keeper. The keeper
ticks in its sleep and pulls

the light in a broad, sensible circle
all night long.
Thought, thought
is hard as a diamond
egg to hatch from.
                    The cormorant's
an old bird: pressed through rock it comes
out the other side,
goes fishing, hangs its wings to dry
in the lamplight. Everything clicks.

Waking

A slow sine wave into day,
surfacing from the aquarium.

The path your eye
insists on,
vertical
to a hushed sweep,
gathering the room into
a known geometry.

Maya at Equinox

Delicate balances have their points of oscillation composed of
a steel knife edge working on agate planes.
  —*Orr's Circle of the Sciences*

If this were the old days she'd
be spinning wool: the last day of
summer, the first
of something she won't name
quite yet, though
the sumacs know, the chicory
poised in their final

reticence know, and name it to themselves
while the sunlight draws its blade
across them. Today the wool
wouldn't stick to her fingers, tacky
with sweat. Nothing new has sounded,

but something old is quiet, suddenly;
she opens her closet, full
of woolen coats from sheep
a hemisphere away.

*

The book she takes from the shelf reads hiber-
nation, Hibernian, *hiver.* The air
still Septemberish: whether
to carry a sweater plagues her for once
more than the planet, that spins
for once not cockeyed.

On the street she repeats the word
equinox.
Through the door of the word,
a hallway.
At the end of the hall, a blue stone.
She's on her way to meet
a man who isn't her lover: her husband.
She spins
a curtain of heavy wool.

*

A woman hangs a blue wool curtain
before a stone.
Nothing new has sounded,

but something old begins to speak,
talking her down the sidewalk as if
she might only fly by instruments
through the clear air. This is the day
the year rocks in its balance,
the equal night. She spins

as the planet spins her. The edge between day
and night, never so honed: split
by the blade she walks both roads, down
the street, down the hallway, toward winter.

from Walking the Borders

PHLOGISTON

Of the campfire we think: oxygen
marries dry juniper, violently,
atom by atom. What is gained
by this bright union,
ash, smoke, our dinner of fried trout.
                 The alchemist
thought of fire: *something is lost.*
Phlogiston. The igneous
humor, the wood's
escaping soul.

As the soul is lost, in a bad bargain.
As the soul is stolen, by a camera,
   by the naming of a private name.
As the soul is thrown from a high window.
It rises from impact.

You stir the fire. We breathe
juniper smoke, oxygen,
adding the gases to our blood.

Coffee

Over coffee I think of him.
He has overheard this rain, or he rains
himself out of sleep, not knowing
what wakes him. He sways
in the kitchen and blinks, one match
flaming past his fingers.
The water in its black kettle
a bird in its covered cage—
a blind where agitation can dissemble
calmly. And the earth-black powder
just ground. A cup of mud, he calls it.
He is careless with his naming
and does not know, even after
coffee, when he tells some truth
and when he lies.
Does he switch on the radio? Does he
turn off the news and listen
instead to the plumbing's
bad digestion? Today I am
not in that room, and cannot say.
Coffee, black coffee. How are my nerves?
The first cup is steady, the second
still as a pond in a cave.
The third begins to stir in my hand,
small mammal at the end of hibernation.
This is a morning like any other,
and here is a way of waking
forewarned into its bitter warmth.

It Snows Out of a Clear Sky
for C.E.C.

Like the chemist's beaker of tricks,
the air: there is nothing there,
and then the spontaneous white
generation of winter in Tucson.
It fills the dry arroyos, caps
the hydra cactus, gathers
in blades on the alien
palms of this desert.
What is the *it* that snows,
hiding in the wings of language?
The snow that can be named
is not the snow
touching the saguaro lightly along
its spines,
jamming the eight-track brains
of the highway tarantulas.
The woman from Los Angeles whispers,
so that's what it looks like,

as what she's learned to recognize
in books as death or the spiral
into silence falls
piecemeal before her.
It snows, as if someone had nudged it
and said,
Talk, or they will not listen.

Invention of the Phoenix

Now for once it is the real bird annulled in flames;
the one we have built goes on breeding.

The phoenix is false,
as a word or a friend
is false. Remember, we made it
from pieces of bird and the idea of fire,
from a bird and our confusion:
      that what is warm can burn.
      That there is an exchange
      in which this is the currency.

And our confusion about the bird
behind its wall of flight: that we
      are sundered by the third dimension;
      that we climb
      only the ladders we see; the bird
      climbs in transparency.

And with the fire: that it comes
      from the other side of the wall of matter.
      It appears to all the senses. We
      have asked it to live among us with
      the dog, the ox,
      and it has refused us.

It is only that we are confused.
We make firebirds, angels, and a bird
with a life span the length
of memory, which burns, and burns again.

The Dogs

are pacing our yards
like sentries. They yelp
clear across night to each
other, planning.
They shiver. The virus
in each of their glinting minds
connects them.

The dogs
wheel through the park.
Already the lawn has grown a tongue
inside their rim of teeth.
It pleads in a green language: Close
your mouths while you chew!
Cover your bare
grins with your paws, be civil,
be mild, be mild.
The dogs hurl forward,
intent on their leader's
tail, invoking
the moon, their chalk Madonna.

They are calling down snow
in the desert, earthquakes,
raking up fields
of tempting bones. The dogs
all dream like early Christians:
their teeth prepare
for the last day.
And what if I dream every night
that my flag is a tail, angry
and useful?
The dream connects.
The stiff hairs exclaim.

For Jean Valentine

MacDowell Colony 1983

Only strike the log
and the fire explodes in it:

beneath it the coals repeat
the catalog of forms the planet

sleeps through: red mesas,
black doorways into the glowing

city, bright masks rehearsing
the possible, the remembered:

this fire eating wood is the earth's
long dream of itself in a small brick

cave, in this cabin framed by January
birches: the living drink light

and the dead give it back
as flame; this book you've left here,

inscribed *with thanks*
as always for the world's

unaccountable shelter,
and your messengers

inside it,
calling the sleeper awake.

This World Begins on a Wharf

shy of midnight.
Under a moon that is almost
full. Yes, shy.
Its light skims a shiver
over the bay,
the light chill

of cold hands.
From here the world purls off
in all directions:
up, into stars,
Orion as always sharp
in the chaos of sparks;

forward, into the bay,
where the sound water beats
out of its body
rushes in, where a still
thick shadow is nothing,
or is the breakwater;

and down, the world stilted
on pilings, over
pale sand, now covered by
some afterthought of the bay,
now revealed,
a screen where the moon

throws timbers, doctored
blueprints, manic carpentry.

There are other bearings,
poor compass. Their names
dissolve into number, the numbers
divide like cells.

This world has just begun
and it fills them all:
breakers, dark storefronts,
panes of glass pooling
the light the length of a narrow
street, what the woman

on the wharf sees abruptly.
Her short hair caught
in a gray scarf,
her hands clumsy in gloves.
She sees so quickly, hears
so much with her skin, her blood,

that all this time her mind
is full of the last world,
the one she left when she stepped
absently up to the wharf
and found herself here.

In the Solar Wind

There is a sleep that tells every
dream as a nightmare: the figures rise up
in a locked room, and it is the world.
And there is a sleep of open windows,
where all dreams unwind
in golden light: clear tea
with the scent of almonds.
If there is something to look on
that does not waver
like mountains in the mirror of a still lake,
like the outline of trees in a light wind,
I have not seen it.
If there is waking.
Here in the thick
afternoon, I do not remember.

*

Love, here is golden tea
in a glass cup. It is hot,
a flashing cylinder.
Hold the cup still and look in:
the future is there,
but not in a Rorschach of leaves.
Steam rises from the tea,
and what begins in this room
continues. To the molecules
every wall is a window.

*

The table he sets the cup on becomes
a story about a table:
It has four legs.
And another:
She rested her head on the table.
And another:
He sat at the table and wondered
if she would appear.

He remembers the table and sets down his cup.
    the liquid is sweet, and
    afterwards, almonds.
The story of the tea fills the air.
It is not finished,
not even in the next room.

*

What does the table become for the child
crouching under the table?
A dungeon, a warren, the oak-grain
stormy an inch from the eye:
the privacy of narration, the
mechanics of hiding.

*

I am sleep, from which everything falls
as the dream rises up.

You cannot hold me,
not even in your strong arms.

I cannot hold you,
though the story might hold us.

One of us chooses to leave,
or what we are chooses:

we have chosen a world
that splinters and shifts,

from molecule to atom
to particle to quark.

Our substance sinks
into its fractured wealth

while we are left behind
in the poverty of our bodies.

*

He stares out the window
past the blue lake
into black woods
and does not see her coming.
There is the path she would take,
brown needles and earth

through the green grass.
He sips his tea and thinks of sleep,
and imagines her sleeping.

*

I could tell you my love is divisible
into need and desire.

That need reduces to past,
desire to present.

That the past is circumstantial,
the present a problem of engineering.

He sets down his cup and wanders
away from the window, into
the privacy of remembrance,
the mechanics of excuse: *when*
I was a child, he begins, and there,
where no one can find him,
the maps unfold in a small boy's hands:
the states, the pastel countries,
the earth—each sheet
drawn from a greater distance,
as if that were knowledge.
The last shows the planets
careening on the solar wind,
the sun's ionic breath.

*

The province where this story unfolds
is a sheet of blue paper.
Brown lines indicate mountains.
The stars of the cities are black,
though they give off light.
In this country a law was uncovered:
we will never need more than four colors
to mark off our borders.
One of them is green.

*

The pale blue is water,
a foreign country.
He knew he had no right to be
so happy, seeing her
floating in a clear sleep.
And so he stopped.
He did not see her coming
down the needle path.
He did not see her at all.

*

When the story has been well told
all tasks are simpler. We have built
so many empty houses; we have made
the roads that lead back to them broad.
When your hand moves to stroke my hair,
what is the distance you travel?

*

I open the chest and find it empty.
I open the door and the light

is aimless in the room and settles nowhere.
I open the book and wait

for the story to begin.
It will take our present and make it pass.

*

She is sleeping, he thinks,
and then he can reach her: his fingerprints
on the air, on empty space.

She is sleeping, like dice in his hand:
twelve chances.

She is sleeping, like a cue ball:
a problem of vectors, complex but foreseen.

*

You are here, listening,
watching me pace.
You will stay to find out
what happens, what happens.
You will want to know why.

I can tell you: the story goes on
and leaves us behind.
The teller forgets,
and the story finds a new tongue, new breath
to ride on.
The listener turns in his sleep
and then he is gone.

*

She is sleeping. She is standing
in the next room and picks up
the scent of almonds.

She has just emerged from the woods
and follows
the needle path down to the lake

where she will
stop to see her face
in the surface of the water.

FROM *LITTLE APOCALYPSE*

Anamnesis

1.

I was reading the tight-throated prose of thesis
and theory this morning, horizontal
clause after clause, the kind
of line you'd see on the monitor after you'd lost the patient,

when the signal drifted, snagged
on another brainwave:
the long swell of memory broke up the page

the way a migraine can,
light on the water and then
the traveling blindness.

And I tasted a name.
I would call it out, if only I could see
his last gesture moving into any other,
                    say,
to roll out of bed and rummage
into the snarl of socks for last night's coffee,
                        the day going forward.

Useless to wake up again
among the ghosts, the dead uneasy with their plotlessness.

2.

Anamnesis, it's called, when forgetfulness is lost,
as when the power fails and a quiet succeeds it,
dog loose in a dark house,

or when I saw him angle a log in the fire, intent
on building strongly and well what was already burning.

It comes through the brain's static,
electrical stutter at synapse,
through the moiré of light crossing light,
through the cracks in the world that signs make,
their arrows, their undoings—

slash through the sky for *not sky*,
through the heart for *not life*—

or it comes from a world undamaged, seamless motion:
the rain a broad lake stretched thin through time,
I am too slow to see it.

Alpha calm, beta, dreamy delta, theta:
the mind wanders from window to window, peering out.
That was a Monarch or Viceroy, not a ragged leaf.
The gust lofted its deep V straight,

as if up a shaft; how does its startled insect brain
spark, filter, make geometry,
when the world moves it?

3.

Nothing for it
but to ride the brain's mantra, even to sleep.
This is the way
I marry my life to my life,
this writing as the rain falls,

the way the rain spins itself loosely
down its spider-silk,
the hand writing *loose* where I
meant to write *lose*.

Now the wind picks up and the firs
all fan and shiver, the same but not the same,
the wind turning them, lifting
at once the roil of needles,
convection and spray.

It has grown so dark that I cannot imagine
fire, color in the black bark;
it has fallen into moments
as weather falls to rain,

the whole of cloud dispersed and moving,
too many to erase, so swift
and everywhere,
no *not* can find them.

Invocation

There was someone loved
I used to talk to,
                    to him, to her,
                    I do not remember,
inwardly,
as the fire speaks to hardwood,
and that softly,
                    susurrus of many voices
                    joining and parting,
each saying I,
each truthful and shifting.

Someone I loved
and spoke to in all my tongues,
                    who listens now
                    though nothing is left inside
but the hearing.
Though who it was has burned away.
And I must call up the others,
                    the loves I can name,
                    to be silenced.

Mondrian's Forest
in memory of Greg Levey, d. February 18, 1991

1. February 19, 1991

Every car drones a radio,
every shop keeps the TV on.

The smart bombs are thinking their way
into Baghdad, on video grids, in primary colors,

and yesterday in the middle of Amherst, a man
drenched himself in gasoline and lit a match.

Next to the body bagged on the Commons,
Peace on a sheet of cardboard, and his

driver's license, safe, and the old oaks
safe, only the grass charred.

Already the papers have found
neighbors willing to say that he'd *seemed depressed*,

someone to call him *isolated*.
Nine Cambodian Buddhists come

down from Leverett in their saffron robes
to pray. Two Veterans of Foreign Wars

heckle over the chants and the slow
gong, a circle of voices on the block of lawn.

2. *Trees on the Gein, With Rising Moon* (1908)

When Mondrian began
his world held rivers and trees, but not

the water's compliance and not
the ash's stillness, for he was in them.

He stood five trees against a red sky;
floated five more

in the mirror of the red river,
all ten wringing their black trunks

into green.
The trees on the water are breaking up,

breaking up, and still remain
trees in the center of their dissolution.

The trees on the bank flame up inside
their heavy outlines:

imagine a death in a man that pushes
first here then there at the lively

pliable skin. The limbs
distend, too full of ripening.

Thick oils eddy and ripple, a slick
on the turbulence of things.

3. Bodhi

Today on the woods trail by Amethyst Brook,
I prayed, *Kuan Yin*. Kuan Yin, enthroned

in the Asian Museum, enormous in limestone.
She who hears the cries of the world,

her spine sheer as a bluff, and both hands open.
I couldn't say if the polished eyes

were open or lidded. *In the new representation,
reason takes first place*, wrote Mondrian,

his labor then to save the trees from the wind,
to rescue his clean strict sight from the eyes

in his head, that saw only through blood.
I'm not one for praying, but somehow the ice

breaking up, the meltwater surge
of the brook gouged her name from my throat,

the way it gouges the bank out from under the trees
and digs bare the root-weave. Not *she*

who answers the cries, Kuan Yin. Not *she who consoles.*
Her body is still, is stone:

She who will not kindle and blaze
when she hears a man burn.

One Man Watches a Horse Race
for C

One man watches a horse race and suffers because his
horse is losing. The second suffers because his horse
is winning; the race isn't over, and anything might
happen. The third who watches has no money on
the race. He sees sweat foam on the horses' leather,
the rictus that flickers through the crowd. Sees even
himself at the rail, caught in the roiling world. He
suffers for the first man and the second, for human
sight and horseflesh.

Still he comes to the races.
Should he stay away, pretend
that there is nothing here to do with him?

Aubade. How Truth Will Out

A slip of the tongue, say
into your mouth, a slip of the finger
when I type

The angel of incidence
is equal to
the angel of reflection. Angel, you fall

on me like light, that I might read the world by you
and love what I read there: accident, incident,
foolscap with an adage in it.

Creation Myths

There is another world,
but it is in this one.
—Paul Valery

Why we make Russian dolls, make Chinese boxes.
Why we wrap the lump of coal gaily at Christmas:
Here. For you. There is another word, but it is in *this one*:
say, *is one*. Say, *son*, what was that planet inside you
we could not fly to?

Why we talk to empty chairs. Why we are mimes
swaying on tightropes laid out on the ground.
Why we fall off.
Say, *on*. Say *so*. There is another gravity
but it is in this one.

Why we lose our keys in the dark and hunt for them
under the streetlight. There is an other
world: we have no permit but we build there.
Say *this one*, say it well enough, it rises up
and even its north windows catch the sun.

Silver

All night the moon examined what the sun had made:
wheatfields, hayfields, fields
of poppies and the wind.

'Take my silver,' the moon said. 'I have paid
into the ocean's pocket too long
without return.'

The silver fell in the wind, and the wind picked it up briefly
then dropped it. The poppies picked up the silver and promised
the moon a harvest of dreams.

'You'd promise the rain a gray hat,' said the moon. 'You'd
promise the mountains a footstool.'
The poppies nodded.

The wheat spilled the silver all through its tassels, pooled it
and tasted, drank deep. 'Thirsty,' it whispered.
'I give you my thirst

and the chalky earth and the crackle of drought.' And 'Thirsty,'
the hay said. 'No, past thirst. I give you the woman
scything me down,

ricking me up late in the field in your full false light.' At that
moment the woman looked up at the moon and thought,
'Cold mirror, release me.

Distance and silver dance with us always, partners not meeting,
strangers not parting—Show me or leave me.'
And thinking, sang. And singing, spent

her penny of future on brightness and longing.
Then the moon, who had never before saved any thing,
took the coin and moved on.

Coelacanth

Monster sleep,
what runs in your trenches, your thought
estuarial, briny or brackish but never fresh.
The tides have passed a law
for the conservation of salt, and since there's salt
in blood there's salt in every wound.
The little crystals bite. The thinking hurts.
Dear monster I

feel for you, would it were otherwise. Here where
river and ocean contend
that river be river and ocean, ocean,
both are mistaken.
Where flow makes churn
and long waves ravel
and the stray coelacanth pops up, says *Uncle*
or *Pass Not* or *Wake Now for monster*

must be alone, I wake, obedient
weary. I dreamed you
had something to tell me.

Who Flies, Who Swims

I have come inside to tell you
the world floats around us,
insolent weeds and grape arbors,
bottles and rust.
Leave me alone to sing,
I will bother no one.
I remember a boy
who danced with a fish.
How can I answer
his mutterings,
that I should remember him
diving there?
He'll dive forever
unless I forego
memory, song,
my fool's-truth lever
under the solidly wrong.
I remember a man
who loved me forever,
so briefly.
I remember a woman
who told him yes
I will love you forever.
She is still singing
and he is gone.
This is not his song.
Soon it will happen.
I am getting older
and breathing thinner
air at this altitude.
Thinner and colder.

The Women on the Ward

I am sitting with a philosopher in the garden; he says again
and again, "I know that that's a tree," pointing to a tree that
is near us. Someone else arrives and hears this, and I tell him:
"This fellow isn't insane. We are only doing philosophy."
—Wittgenstein, *On Certainty*

1. Lena

hears voices, as I do
now, in memory hearing her rant
and sputter in the treatment room,
shouting that she is good
that she did not.

They come at her from above,
as all voices come to a child.
She lifts up her fiftyish face
and curses,
as they deserve,

tells them the truth of it,
the goddamn unheard truth of it,
that never changes.
Adamant dead with their

stopped clocks, they say
I am right I am right
twice a day.

2. Diana

Who dresses Diana every morning,
from the waist up,
from the waist down?
In the name of the moon goddess,
virgin and hunter,
every day the same, she wears
her schoolgirl cardigan and A-line skirt,
the pressed blouse buttoned high,
and down below,

blue satin evening pants
and gold high heels.
On the nights before electroshock
she would know these stories;
teaches, she sometimes remembers,
at a women's college;
has studied the patchwork
hippogriff, the sphinx and chimera,
their bodies wrenched together
from warring kingdoms.

Knows more than I have known.
Until I saw her
straighten her sweater at the full-length mirror,
adjust her cuffs and smile
her bland satisfied smile,
I'd never known, reading the ancient stories,
that the lion-bodied woman haunting the city gates
accosted passersby to ask
her winged, carnivorous riddle artlessly,
just wanting an answer.

3. The Telling

I saw her fly out of the swing
and through the air, says the mother.
She landed on that rock. But she got up.

Standing and almost conscious, the child totters.
In her head the house blinks off and off,
the backyard shatters.

When there is nothing to see, she hears
a tightwire sing in her brain.

She takes a step
into the strobe of sunlight,
walking, she thinks, walking toward
her mother at the kitchen door,
the woman motionless, watching.
The child falls at the foot of the stairs.

The mother shrugs.
I thought she was dead, so I left her there.
And there is something in her voice—
something wry and satisfied,

something shapely and final her daughter bows to,
thinking one day she will know the point of this story,

the telling familiar, repeated to cousins and in-laws,
burnished and cryptic as a fairy tale,
as if the story had happened to some other child.

4. Kelly Jo

Four teeth lost to Snake's, her boyfriend's, backhand,
she fingers the gap in her grin and keeps
her good eye on me, her cast eye scanning
always *over there*
on the border of her vision.
Schizophrenic, antsy
for the nurse on rounds with the meds cart,
My Candy Man, she calls her, chanting
that ain't no woman, even in a girdle,
Kelly Jo cruises
the hall that is her corner
this week, next week she's going home.

She wants her Con-tr-r-r-olled Sub-stance, says
this ward is a day at the bitch! after
the Psych Center where they make you strip
with the male aides watching.
She's aching for her rye, her coke,
'ludes melting her bones to wax
in the good hot sun; wants her
teeth back, wants her Snake,
shy, palms me the poem she made

for Deley down the hail, who cries.
Pretty face, it starts, *and smart*
They got you anyway.

When JJ, on Prolixin, starts his ritual brawl
in the sunroom—
when the aides maneuver, watchful as coyotes,
one out front to take his feints, two
dropping behind to pin him
face down, the carpet burning his cheek,
Kelly Jo finds her burrow behind a vinyl sofa.

She is seeing all that she knows
and whimpers it faster and flatter than speech,
don't let him hurt me, until
the tremors exhaust her. All touch is pain,
so I circle my arms and rock the air around her.
Then she grins again, the Dalmane coming on,
her hand a beat too late to hide her teeth,
the tattooed snake on her shoulder shrugging
the rose in its mouth.

5. Cassie

A shadow world, a world of light:
philosophy that doesn't bruise the clouds
the way the rain does. She sees them
cluster past the grated window,
sky in a grid, Cartesian gray.

Her body dances without her, one foot
tapping in 5/4, a shoulder
jerking in waltz time, the Stelazine
samba. Hard to hold the brush, harder
to guide it to the orange paint,
to catch the oriole, its tic-tac-toe,
one square at a hop. Undivided
intention, the matter. Unsplit,
the light is colorless.

It is not possible to lie, only
to tell the truth she wants is knotty.
She wants it for herself, the one
that will not disappear
like all the others when she looks away.
The massy paint. The canvas field.
And if the gravity holds,
and if the flat absorbs the random light
and lets the color out, the one
cord of it that binds her here,
that is enough.

6. Susan

—They tell me I'm dying, but I don't believe it.
Know why? Some Fridays
I drive to the mountains—
after the four-lane ends the road
is a spiral staircase, the car
skates up like a plane on a runway,
I always think wings. And then I start thinking
which light I've left burning, or what window's
open. In the woods, in my tent, with the owls
spooking and tree shadows raining
small moons on the ground,

I keep seeing my house
lit up all night—or worse, all day,
like a match in the sun.
I feel like I'll never get back.
But here, when the nurses quit fussing,
I sleep. I don't stop to worry
what lights I've left burning,
what light's burning out.

From The Dictionary of Improbable Speech

telson *n.* as far as you can go. To the limits of sound. [macaronic, from Greek *tel*, far, and Latin *son*, sound.]

1) The point at which bats refine a word into an instrument of echolocation, so that a single utterance can locate the speaker in the three dimensions of the physical world and reveal every gnat and twig and human obstacle in its path, so resonant and enduring that the bat-speaker can use it to navigate from the place it was spoken to the place where a new word can be said.

2) The point at which one of a pod of dolphins mutters a single not untranslatable but still unprintable word into the ocean and finds the whale-watch boat, at which they interrupt dinner and even sex to woo the humans on board, doing their profoundest diplomatic duty on behalf of their homeland, delighting the poisoners with honor, making first a hieroglyphic for play, and then a rebus that says

leap up

plus

dive down

equals. . . .

3) The other side of the equals sign, where the bipeds listen for the rest of the equation.

LUCID DREAMING: A BOOK OF HOURS

ONE

in the morning—odd that this fulcrum rests
in the middle of darkness. Heliotrope, solar top,

the earth rolls us into the glare, out
of our duncecap shadow—by the numbers, not like

the cloud's slow wheel to rain, slurry,
river, ocean; nor even the men in their travels,

always returning. One sleeps behind the wall
and swims the white sheets that fold and twist

in the leftover light. Here on the dock, I have the water.
Or rather, what I have is its skin, that catches

red and green from the harbor lights,
and the waves that pass through it and leave it

whole, in their decorous physics,
and the hollow bass of the foghorn drilling me

clean of chatter. I think it must start
the octave of his sleep, pulling the neurons'

improvisations, the all-night REM fugue,
back to this tonic. That far, we are together, two,

and three, in the next house, and four,
five, in the bounty of counting.

AND THE TWO GIVE BIRTH TO THE MYRIAD OF THINGS

—said Lao-tse, sage of waterfalls, who

knew how the courtly heart keeps trying the world.
Heart wants only the good: dreams like a glass

harmonica, ringing light's measures. Love like art
if art could grow from seed, unfolding the code

inside it. But what the mind has sundered
cannot stay long uncluttered. Innocent heart, I

think, good heart, it wants, wants just now good
hands to coax my shoulders loose. What are we

birthing, when one thing leads to another,
two swimming the body's heat together?

If you want to know how the Way makes
a world, desire. But if you want to know the Way,

want nothing. A tall order, either way, worse
in the wanting not to want, as if desire can only

redshift like the galaxies who fly from us, who never
knew us. The distant water insists on falling inward,

to earth, to hell with all the stars retreating around us. O
Lao-tse, o Hubble, o love. It all comes down

to the ocean, in time, singing more deeply
the farther it travels. Its bass line thrums

the floorboards, the walls, such slow decay I can't
feel the dust on my skin until he is sleeping.

TRIPTYCH

Sun horse, night mare,
Ride what you find there.

i

Three minutes, no longer, in this cold ocean, you no longer feel
the margins of your body; contracted but whole,

your nerves reporting back from a shrinking perimeter,
you think you are swimming, homunculus,

but the limbs don't answer. The skin out there is gone, that divided

water from water. Sleep by the ocean's a double solvent.

The soul swims out of the body and joins salt and the isolate tidal
life of cells. Diatom, rotifer, I was a colony. Now they are free.

The ocean pants like a big cat next to our bed.
The dream it made is gone. Body, be still, be safe, it's just

adrenaline's druggy buzz, a homemade panic
the nerves cook up in the dark, their boredom.

ii

The sun on my skin where I met the world, the light I read
his face by, touch, the whole

of what I saw and did not see, now, at 3 a.m.
draws back to the marrow and burns. Who said

the conscious mind is like a flashlight? Whatever
it looks at is bright. This is a glowing universe, it thinks,

what's real is light. But the ocean I didn't attend to is in
my nerves, the stitch in my ankle partway up the cliff

trail, and Muzak and the riverrun of breathing,
all kindle in the cells. His short laugh burns there, and the water's

purr, and our bodies loose to gravity. I want to tell him,
love, on this planet, we wake on the beast's back,

dream of its waking. By morning, at breakfast, I will not
remember, and now he is sleeping.

iii

Three minutes, one hundred-eighty seconds—each
divisible as light, as shades in the water,

so long, the blade of moonlight opens
a shallow trough into greens the eye

could study all night,
if the body could stay here.

Sparking and tacking in deeper blues,
the mind works its perfect doll of a swimmer.

FOUR

Eye travels out to the headland, black sphinx couchant
on the night's field; then over the harbor, horizon lit

from below by invisible Boston; finally rises, to Venus,
to Altair. Wherever I look in the beautiful box of space,

an effortless journey. The fourth dimension is time—
just try to see through it. Too late to sleep, says the peevish

clock in my brain. Sleeping, says body, deep in night's
furrow. It comes and it goes, says his breathing beside me.

Once I imagined Einstein's time as a track made of light
that the space-train followed,

going somewhere, the wake of its going
still bright behind us. Yes, I remember.

FIVE O FIVE

says the insect light of the digital clock,
and in the leaching dark I watch him sleep,

his eyes turned inward, his walk begun
down the nerve-lit alleys of his body.

I dream that he dreams a boy flying over
the ochre fields and the tumbled corpus

of foothills, both father and mother, the tangled
landscape of his making, lifting

now into wind-chipped mountains, outcrop and spire.
He starts, as at a rattlesnake, starts

noticing, starts listening
to the slow music the rocks tease out

from the tuned columns of air.
Art, we call it, the old

second person singular *to be*,
its *thou* still intimate and absent.

Would it be better love
to stop dreaming him? In somnia. In gray exile,

better only to praise
his solitude where I cannot follow.

From there, airborne in sleep, the river
etches the valley with a branching tree. Its delta

is the sky, where the first green reaches when
the sun strikes. Its current returns him, rocks him to wake

in his breathing; landlocked in his
skin now, bone-bound at my side, he opens his eyes.

SIX OF ONE,

half a dozen of the almond biscotti, the cappuccino
steaming. Love demands good food and some small

crime against the sensible. It says this morning
we are not poor, this morning is a cul-de-sac

off the main drag. The sun rising burns the harbor
open, ignites the gulls to feeding; one long thin cry pierces

another; offshore wind bends sound so sharply
it meets itself coming and going, tangle of sound and

blown-away ravel of night's knots into morning.
I tell him I stayed awake but not

that I spent those hours in orbit around his sleep like some
derelict planet, careening toward his dark side,

never catching up. From orbit we've seen the terminator
travel like rain on the prairie: wall of sunlight

whose top is lost in heaven,
whose clean hard edge advancing

ruffles no leaf and translates
being into being. What did you

dream? I ask, and he says
I was with him all night,

that he dreamed what was real,
all that I wanted to hear.

SEVEN

for luck, and for the seven heavens, transparently stacked
like an archaeological dig into glassworks; we say broad

daylight, but it's also deep. I want to find the stratum where
virtue is pure description: the virtue of mercury

is speed. The virtue of the soul is joy. Break a thermometer
and mercury, so rapid and silver it seems to ride on light,

shatters into mirrors of itself: identical beads, all whole,
all fleeing. The mind's virtue is difference; the heart's,

sameness—deeper than before, this resonance, this tide's
diastole and pulse. The body, in its obstinate formality,

plain under the blue vault endlessly lifting, heavy on the
warming sand—the body's virtue is renewal. Cell after cell

it loses all that it has, and still goes on,
faithful amnesiac lover of the sun,

the sun that says *I have not left*,
that says *I have returned.*

EASTPOINT. CODA

Without explaining how I came to stand here
counting the boats in the harbor and losing count

every time the tide changed, so that I could have
marked off each day by its lapse of attention;

without telling the Freudian, astrological, accidentally
fateful plots; without atoning for, without retreating from

the tenderness spent on green leaves, white pages,
the absolute black of the alphabet—

so that the hours rested on stilts of words and the words
like the turtle who holds up the world, stood

on the currents of space, on nothing—
without warnings or forecasts;

I want to show you this beach, the violet
light cast up by the ocean, and something

that Einstein never saw: a space
that isn't married to time:

open water, without boats

briefly, until they come home.

Sense, Sensed

The fox in the field is a standing wave,
a graph of attention.
Then he breaks for cover. The wave snaps flat
into red direction.

~

A dancer is the patron saint of trust.
The poet is a saint of hesitation.

~

Even the spidery bare
branches I want to call tangled are tangled
only by distraction.
Closer. They unclench.
Small unhurried rivulets of tree.

~

I work to be changed,
or someone like an I,
though hardly enough to interrupt a mirror.

~

Can't leave them
where they lie: shells and stones
on the beach, their pearl and uranium light—

inert on the desk as any gravel, still,
touched in their shallow dish they're cold
as the unmade, fade
more slowly than roses.

~

The poet bends in language like
a rose in its bud vase,
green stroke of its stern alive and

broken at the water line,
shifted away from itself at the point
where water baffles the light.

~

And the moral of this book,
my friend once said,
is 'don't kill yourself.'
The moral of most books, this one included,
is *Look what happens if you don't.*

~

Poets have voices the way mountains have hermits.

~

The adepts of experience
practice practice.

Remember the match that burns twice,
a child's courtship with pain,

the firewood that warms twice,
an adult's joke on effort.

~

I worked to be changed,
was changed into something
that no longer worked.

~

Poetry, for
solitude loves boundary.

Solitude, the word wrapped around its
contraband quiet.

~

For poetry is sense, sensed.
There is nothing to Ariadne but her thread.

~

A woman walks down a hall in her house:
a wall has disappeared, where yesterday
her photographs, diplomas,
portrait hung. What shall we call it,
this tunnel blind-sided by space, where she stands?

~ ~ ~

Like the Second Hand on a Very Slow Watch

The moon goes brassy as it sets behind us.
It is March, after midnight,
and we are easily two hundred, frozen idiotic
at the ferry's railings, deck stacked on deck
like a cake Edmund Halley might jump out of
when his comet comes forth, if it does.
I'm an habitual tourist on these waters.
I come here to spy
on the privacy of whales,
humpbacks named Petra and Cassiopeia, and Dud,
the aging calf still shadowing his mother.
They always appear, though some days
only in the distance. And the comet
shows up now too, as a faint scar of light
under Sagittarius. From out past the orbit of Pluto
it ticks toward the sun,
in photos like Muybridge's galloping horse,
stopped, stopped—
and up in the wheelhouse Zeno's ghost
clocks the cartoon frames and mutters,
It's not only motion that's illusory. Some
infinities are so small we couldn't trip over them.
Some words,
like *infinity*, are trap doors the mind
disappears through. Even now,
convened in wind above the frigid
water, under heaven,
our little post-druidical navy
keeping vigil outside Boston Harbor,
we pass the binoculars, think
perhaps the mystery hasn't begun.

Calling & Singing

Brownian clouds of blackflies,
and pine needles silver as Persian cats
in the afternoon sun—

even the chickadee is horny,
one ounce of sex and a shrill
seesawing two-note

all through May,
month named for contingence
and supplication.

By July that amorous
tape-loop shuts down; he's left
for the rest of the year with nothing

to say but his own name,
over and over, from the one nest he gets
in all this forest.

Eve, Before

The great trees labor
and bring forth blossoms.
The lazy, the self-forgetful kingdoms,

from angels and beasts
down to the rocks and mica-eyed
insects, leave them to their work,

the making of sticky
fruit and sweet
juice out of light and earth.

This is no food chain,
only food—
for we precede the birth of justice;

the rain falls equably on us
and no one gets wet,
except for the otters

who dive in its caresses,
because they are the shape that water took
and loved best.

The sky grays only to sharpen
the fern's greens; the sun
breaks in just as we are thinking

we'd like to see the magenta
petals more clearly, and the blue aura
their color excites around them.

We are bare monkeys, I tell him,
but he has his own
names for what he finds in the tangle

of branches. He chatters and points
through the canopy where the parrots
husband their nests and the snakes

glide away on the limbs from something
that hasn't happened.

Frond

That which opens its hand but grasps
nothing, cradles without drinking
the globe of water last night
left it, amulet
that holds the sun now
rising, and who could discard it?

That which blooms from its wrist
like a green fist
and then finds peace. Its twin
unfurls, on the same stem,
in the same breeze.
Applause. Applause.

Drosophila

Red eyes, white eyes.
In this classroom in
America,

fifteen-year-olds with their seed
swarming in their ovaries and balls
study the long Mendelian

lottery: the politics of chromosomes,
of dominance and
the recessives banding together

to be heard.
They peer at the hairy articulations
of thorax and legs, and score:

red, white, red, onto the grid
of begats, the bulky
entomological novel

that traces the curse unto the thirtieth
generation. One girl
sneaks from the cafeteria to the lab,

smuggling her fruit salad in
a dixie cup, and watches
the seethe grow sluggish in the sticky slough

of maraschino cherry.
She is counting on mutation,
on breaking the chain of the law and making

compound eyes of topaz,
eyes like star sapphire, jade eyes
that look back in recognition.

Frog. Little Eden.

Amphibious, at home
on the surface

tension, in
over my head, not
out of my depth, not deep
deep deep,

not in far. Not
high and dry, not
even in treetops,
where I sing water
into the root-hairs.

It seeks me, will not
forsake me.
Hand over hand it climbs.
It breaks
the first law of water,

all for my song.
Into the trunk and up, it greens
the leaves that the leaves may be
-emerald me.
The leaves breathe it out and I drink,

then sing

lest the water forget to rise
and the world be kindling.

Lot

Come out of the city by I-95
in the center lane: passed left,
passing right bubble after
bubble-world, an elbow out or driver's
palm cupping the wind,
giving like a kite a moment, human
limbs that make the flight
a bird-migration, mind, mind,
mind not by communion curving here
but publishing the shape of space

for who might read it. Tract gives way
to field, to waste, but how the road banks
on this S makes a new *down*,
meets my G's securely.
Mountains soon. Scrub here,
as only farms could make it,
having failed. One tree ahead
is humpbacked under vine, behind
and gone; sunflowers buckle
under their seed-heads.

Half the weeds out there
are medicine or food,
even the kudzu whose root
thickens ginger sauce and cools a fever.
Proves nothing, except we are not
special, that chemistry describes us,
suggests we are not aliens on the earth,
despite our foreign manners.
Weed eats what weed gets. Bach
dopplers by, at 80 barely cruising.

At Tanglewood
for Melinda Wagner & Jim Saporito

The reason these musicians gather
in a shell—far from the sea,
in hills where ammonites dream dry
compacted geologic dreams
about the water, lover that left them—

the reason they cradle oboes and flutes
against their summer whites,
or cross the stage and hover
over piano and harp, those harder
life-sized lovers who waited—

and that the harpist closes
around her gilded frame
and grazes the strings—
is that the shell opens out
to the lovers here on the lawn,

and that it arches back on itself,
around the germ of its thinking,
that in this spot-lit nest,
as the music escapes it, each little
I can brood on itself and so go on.

From The Dictionary of Improbable Speech

sorus *adj.* of any cloud that makes sound—that breathes, sings, intimates, gasps—as it gathers and condenses. Commonly known as *whisperers*, sorus clouds form from nimbus clouds that refuse to rain; what the sorus clouds mutter depends largely on why the rain would not fall. If the cloud could not seed because the air was swept clean by a cold wind, the sorus cloud says *brrr, were, cur.* If the nimbus could not rain because the air around it was dry, its daughter sorus says *xeric, pyrrhic, sick.* Both litanies have dire effects on the fauna on the planet's surface. But a raincloud that delays its outburst of water for the sheer love of water becomes a sorus that whispers *hold, mold, unfold.* And love climbs its ladder.

Saguaro National Forest

Caliche. Fissures
run and branch,
shot veins in the eye or the set
of all rivers photographed from orbit.
The track water takes, then leaves.

Just now, in Sonora, it's leaving
before it arrives: *ghost rain*
falls, the air drinks it.
It shimmers in the heat's throat.
Is this where *forest* ends,

a word in its dotage?
In the long-lobed yoga of cactus
groundwater wells.
The cactus draws it
up to the flower hidden in its skull,

waiting to open, past patience.
Eighteen feet in the air, its arms
were flailing when the world stopped.
In a forest, that would have been
prayer, or anger,

a melee of leaves
in their transpiration.
But saguaro grows always more singular.
One here. One here.
Each sits with its taproot sunk

to the water in the back of the desert's
mind, and drinks back, remembering.

Mystic

comes from *Missituck*,
> Mashantucket Pequot for
>> *where the little river joins the ocean.*

Same thing. A wetter
> baptism than some would like.
>> The ink runs, it smudges the type

of the law's letter. The boats belly
> their pregnancies by wind across
>> the water; no shame; no whales

anymore rendered of their large
> minds in oaken vats.
>> Better a museum, and it is.

Its parking lot is Jaguar country,
> Acura, Mercedes, foreign plates.
>> Casino's north, where pilgrims

finally pay. Sheep bleat among boulders
> bigger than sheep. Egrets
>> in salt marsh. Deer

the land won't feed this drought year
> calm as horses on the lawn. Who
>> would ask for justice?

The ospreys could not
> fold their six-foot wings around
>> a wind like that.

>>> —*Mystic, Connecticut, 1996*

The Restorer

Dionysus and the Lynx   mosaic at Delos

Where brush's bristle touches,
damage blooms. What can I
unearth? Naked plaster,
fractal as seacoast,
eats at the rocks: here his body
born from his father's
thigh, all muscle and come-drench;

there a bearded lynx head yawns
in its wreath of bracken,
cat-mask at wood's edge.
She-cat, prey-bait. God-trap, there,
the shattered tiles make her.
She will land in a puddle of birds like a stone.
When the spray clears,
who will remain?

Unearth. To heaven or that strict place
I have in mind, called sight.
This god has the full red lips of a woman,

wings too small for his gravity.
His hunters skein through
blue woods behind him, their bullroarers slung
to wring murder's axioms out of the air
when the sign comes. He makes no sign,
looks pouty and fretful.
Perhaps the wine has not arrived,

perhaps he might be late for the job of his madness.
The dark grout reads as shadow,
deepens his eyesockets, coarsens his skin,
who is immortally dissolute.

The lynx belongs to Aphrodite.
He has almost seen her.
One more eye-beat and he will read
a pair of eyes and ear-tufts and a grin
within a cat, her signature.
If I were drunk with wine or love
I'd pluck his eye out, so, a clumsy
chip would do it.
                    Tile's
a dirt that burned quickly.
The dirt on the tile has done
its tedious burn in the air, and what's

to choose between them now?
No matter. Love looks out.
Her animal face is not
the mask I thought it was.
Under the grime the god
is golden like retsina, and
makes drunk. His men are mad
and his quiver flares with infallible
arrows. The cat hunts too,
and soon a thing
great and winged will pass her.

The News from Mars

*"... the diaspora of human civilization is bound to go on
and out, as it always has done in the process of setting new
frontiers."*
—Gerard K. O'Neill

1. Earth

The sky buzzed as always with its crossing traffic.
Then came the flash, a last photograph
before we disappeared, in negative color:

    red trees reflected in the orange pond,

    the roses cool blue holes
    in the garden's fire,

    and the cloud, blossoming chastely
    like an unused sun coming up.

This quiet. This unimagined.
It was a dream stolen from a movie.
Even in sleep I had no other language
for it but film,
the art of light, light's preservation,

and broken from sleep I am
crazy with this fiction.
This morning the world has not ended,
is not transfigured.
Streetlights dim in the gray sky. The garish
dream lights blink out, in room after room
of this city block.

2. Off-planet: Mars

The horizon-line clear and arched as an orange.
Above it, blackness with stars, the faint
enormous corkscrew of the galaxy. Below it,

all ground is foreground. Every lazy step
reels more of the world in. Think of

Nijinsky, who told the reporter, *Just leap
into the air, and pause a little.*

Our heads are heavier than our hearts,
as we'd always suspected.

The two moons cross in the sky,
and the doubled shadows merge:

at my feet, then trailing
my drifting body, the black
body of a woman, foreshortened
and sexless in her bulky suit.
My breath is a storm in my helmet, and what
I see, I see through it.

3. Earth: Night Fallen

Through my window, with its glass
flowing year after year
into the base of its frame,

Mars is a dull red spot hanging over the warehouse,
and all I imagine about it begins

it is not like this: no rain trapping
the light on the surface of the black street;
no street. The movie must have ended
with the good people helping each other, the bad

looting and double-crossing and dying badly.
The good die well, or stand
brave and elegiac against the ruined backdrop.

At the Synchrotron Lab

In the sunlight of the upper world, the bookkeepers sit,
and the secretaries, over mugs of coffee—
mugs with red hearts or Japanese
irises on their long stalks, mobius brushstrokes.

She is plump, twenty-three. They are planning her wedding,
the bridesmaids in turquoise. No, coral. The flowers.
The professor asks her type, and she does:
lambdas, omegas, the beta a B on its rocking tail.

Her skill is so sharp in her fingers she thinks
the new house   the man's bed   the money   the child
the next step   and makes no mistake.
Downstairs they're arguing voltage and money,

and the quarks in their colors and flavors: *up, down,*
charm, strange, truth, and beauty, real
as love or numbers, true
as a fable. Like this one: a woman walks over the earth

with a lamp, looking for One. She looks in the sky
as it blues and darkens. She looks in the whorl of a geode,
she looks in the satin ear of a shell,
in a mole's stunned eye, in the alleys of the capital,

and she is unafraid. If she finds it, she can seek Two.
Here, under the field with its harsh cropped grass,
the magnets rest in their tunnel.
They are painted the primary colors of code, red, yellow,

blue, for they steer the invisible. Electrons shoot clockwise.
The positrons, their mirror image, double negatives,
fly widdershins into *annihilation*—
that is their word now, and the blade of their precision.

The little apocalypse repeats and repeats. I can see it
in the dials, in the needles swinging. The digits roll up
in their windows. This lab
is full of the paraphernalia of light—the spectroscope,

oscilloscope, the meters and glassy lucite cable
coiled on the workbench like a failed basket—
to hold the flash that comes
when the matter breaks open, and whatever the numbers

say about the world. Is it only that the world
is in the numbers, in the tracks through a cloud chamber?
And in this probing: what I close
my hand on, name, forget. Then want again.

LATE POEMS: FROM *FAR GOOD*

Far Good

So far, so. A little song. In Istanbul the jeweler flicks a tiny elephant, an agate ring. "If it's in the heart, it goes easily to the wallet." He waxes large on the coming together of peoples, Europe, Asia, for the sale.

The heart isn't a wallet & it wasn't in the wallet. We tasted a pepper so hot it took three men to serve it, one for the dish, one for the glasses, one for the water with lemon.

At breakfast, silk rosebuds flecked with wax dewdrops.

On the island I burn on olive oil, cheaply, like a lamp. Here it's the long thought of living one atop the other, the tinder floors and ceilings, the wax. More men could serve us.

The wallets are stuffed with 10,000 lira notes for bread and coffee. We slept at the Hotel And, and the headboard remembers us. No one else.

Someone yelled in perfect English when we passed his stall, "Why not? I'm not Freddy Krueger, I'm not a terrorist."

Little, so late, the word we wait for. And. And.

Grapes

Red grapes.
Seedless red grapes
born from vines cut
and always twice removed.
Frosted in July by the white box
in the kitchen, the one electricity
pulls the heat from, not the one
that puts heat in. So sweet
from so far away, so far so good.

When Penelope Sailed

Late night, I wake and slip it on.
It burns so.
I switch it to the widow's
finger. Heavy as plutonium
my right hand's not my own.
Life starts too late and ends
so soon that no eye bends
one arc of the moon.

Half Boat

The coffin runs aground. Only the prow,
all intentions, beached on the other shore, the souls inside
who paid their passage are free as fish in the first
amnion. No judgment for the blessed
who swim like this.

Here there's a wind. In
another room it's still. Still
windows open, close.
Suppose the walls were blank, banks
of blindness against the chill.

Kombolói

Learning again to worry the beads,
loose wrist and light catch, ease
in the camel bones as silk wraps the hand
in almost silence. My last strand
was heavy glass, green
darker than olives or the sea and caught
every light and made loud shakerie.
I like this softness, no flash
to tell the block
the troubles now grown old.

Bourbon with Petrarch

If you can taste the oak in aging love,
then no betrayal overcomes the taste
of smoke on the lips and fire in the throat.
You drank some drug that no blood test can trace.

Love asks every thing, but will take nothing
for an answer. How you savored feta,
olive oil, oregano. Your wit rang
a blue note in sullen America.

And if you're gone, I'm not. The love goes on.
It has its own life, eating through the heart,
and heart eats all the world, the sight, the sound,

the scent you left, that I might track you by,
the road we staggered drunkenly to art.
Open your hand. Let you fly, let me fly.

WENDY BATTIN

Geometry 1

Courage: the heart times time

Silence:

Reason: a program

Helix: one body climbing a staircase

Matter: is dark, or light, or

Weightless: the thing that escapes when the earth lets go

Frogs shrill as April high in the trees

GPS

How many places must we live
Or unlive, before we are home.
               —Anna Husain

In my 60th year I awoke in a bright place, where trees
had never grown. It was a raft, I think, or a tangle
of Sargasso. Currents not current, only the kelp
in long strands netting me there. How
the pods float, ready to seed, how motion
lost its compass. If there's no place to go,
stay here. You'll stay and go, says the tangle
of lives, one way or another.

Ten Things You Don't Know About Me

1. I am not a ghostwriter. I'm a ghost, writing.
2. I live in a box in a box on a block.
3. And, in Istanbul, it was The Hotel And where the bed broke.
4. I'm fluent in one language, viscous in two, and sludge in three. In the others I'm solid.
5. The sun is in the corner of my eye.
6. Lately my ribs say Enough! and my wrist says Too Much! All my body is quoting Blake.
7. That was the cat you heard last night. Not me.
8. He was singing Kyrie eleison. I didn't teach him that.
9. Dear reader, it's always been you.
10. I know the secret of eternal life: when you take your last breath, hold it, as a diver holds out for the pearl. Now it's yours.

OTHER LATE POEMS

The Ferry Lies Down on a Sharp Rock

as if a taxi found a cliff in Manhattan
heretofore unknown   therefromaft   water
bone cold

the octopus like a softball in its mitt

Naxos with its doorway into nowhere: two
columns, one
lintel, either way you look it's world, more world.
The drowned there too.

It's true. There's been a rock with a doorway on it
for three thousand years.

Why does the argument go on.
Why can't someone walk through.

An Asterisk Named Fred Astaire
for Halvard Johnson

Star descending a staircase, five-pointed,
at least when clothed. In his tux, he is,

made all of plasma, super-
fluid and hot. Another cool that burns. The first

has no legs, will not endure: it's not a work of arc,
no asterism. I have a cold that burns me up.

Or flu. Fred cascading
ramifies in fever's eyes.

The squirrels are playing
walnut-soccer, it's October, on the roof. The cat is mad

domestic. He fields it all through glass but doesn't
have the physics for it: reflex over 2

divides the will. Fred, on the other foot,
and just those two, behind the glass wall touches down

like a spacesuit on the moon,
inhabited, but only just.

Christmas in Connecticut

Not what you think. Rain.
The cards are all in Greek.
The man unwraps a joke in the box.
The woman unwraps

a silver man with the head of a bird.
They are so in love, the four of them,
the man the joke the woman the beaked
aluminum dream,

they laugh at the eyes, the leg, the ear,
the arm all hung in the tree.
Two headless torsos,
his and hers, twist in the branches.

See how the world is made new?
Whatever I tell you is true.

Brief

The light goes. The light comes back.
Sleep in winter. I will sleep beside you
for the warmth, the other face of light,

which will be back, bang on the pans
or not. I lit the tree tonight and read
the gold and blue lights on your face.

We go and come. I cannot hold you
but I hold you for the warmth. The other side
of that is dark but touch will take us.

Clown with Drum

Clown with Drum, Walt Kuhn, 1943

Canvas wears paint as land wears its rivers, as hanger
wears shirt if the shirt is silk. A clotheshorse her mane.
Not this clown. He grins as
I write, by unwriting. His paint wears him.
He lives in a room with the door painted shut.
Someone inside
might touch the skin of the drum, someone

hollow in the drum
might speak: stroke of the mallet, a sigh.
Throw the arm wide for the crowd and strike,
thunder in Asgaard.
Or it's only ruffle and grin, no one's in.
                                        Just
that the hands are painted bare, his hands are there.
Conundrum he might make some sound from, rhythm
even, though the weight says no. Square as pages, every part of him,
and on a heavy world, say Jupiter. Does the soul
grow blowsy in the suit it's called to fill
or does the will
bide until the paint is dry, the painter's back
is turned, then rise and burn?

Museum Piece

1.

Since each woman has a history conjured
out of repetition, no one
crosses the gallery to her when she says

I can't bear the flowers on the table,
the light painted in through the missing window.
The visitors stand at the canvas as if
at a door they consider opening,
then turn away.

2.

And here the painter wonders,
what does a young girl do with herself
in the morning?
He has provided the window
she does not look out.
She sits wholly wrapped in a flowered
quilt, and the back-light gathers in her hair.

3.

Think of this kind of boredom, nursed
in the house of objects:
the woman combing her hair,
combing her hair. The blinds are lowered
for her headache, raised when she thinks the moon
has risen, lowered again.

4.

The woman is dressed to be well-behaved.
If she keeps talking, the guards will come.
If she keeps silent the crowd
will flow around her, then go home.

Liberty

She turned every tap in the house: fire.
Fire in the shower. Fire in the sink.

He parked at the trailhead and could not walk.
Thou shalt not thou shalt not

slit the throat of the radio. A dream. She wakes
and washes and is not burned. He drives

and the news makes the road
he drives on, where else could he go?

Mercy 1

In the past tense. *We were.* Noticed
not much. Loved as profession,
our children all our resumé. He said,
I don't think I should open your letter.
Who knows what sickness waits inside.
But let me tell you the moth on my door
had blue-green eyes. Had dried beech wings,
as if it had studied trees and chosen.
Patient under the magnifying
glass, that I might know it.
Let me look at you, at first from a distance.

Triangula
for Pam, Joan, Laura & Mary Jo

Bright stars kite above cloud scud,
two blue-white, one red.
Falling upward into the black
triangle I think,
not Cassiopeia, not Cepheus, not Draco,
dragon-scaled tail snaking over the Pole,
not the Big Dog, or Camelopardalis
(and which fond god hoisted
a baffled giraffe
into the heavens?
Knock-kneed and mute,
unable to whicker its protest?).
Not Cygnus or Andromeda.

Call it Triangula, three-winged
insomniac bird: iridescent, many-eyed
and bleary as a peacock's tail,
spiraling always inward
like a rower with one oar.
Dream-deprived he dreams awake,
the universe his long hallucination
in the night. Isosceles, acute,
obtuse, but not quite right
after all these eons,
he keeps his strict geometry
but loses track of details.
Where is his mate, for instance,
those three glimmers
mirrored in the water, wavering seductively
upon the swells? In the arms of Morpheus,
no doubt, the snoring hussy.
And under which wing could he tuck his head
and leave us to a saner god?

Mir, the World, or is it Peace,

circles the planet waiting to come home. So long,
the cold. There was a silence, and I thought me gone.
Blind as numbers I would lay me down
in India or Indiana, fire works.

On New Year's Eve, fire will work for food.
But now the earth is talking back again

and tells me, robot on a little longer.
He who doesn't robot doesn't eat,

not even potatoes, not if fire's licked them.
So this is how the world goes on. You count

and someone tells you, go on counting.
After the flash, Two

thousand and one. Two
thousand and two. Till you hear the thunder.

The Dead

made what they could of it: flight, and music, sporadic
explosions. More dead, for company. Babies.
Seventeen kinds of arches and keystones. Engineering

and yoga. Anthropology. What you might wear in summer
and winter, and how to weave it. Where the fish are.
Where the fish are. Where to drop our nets.

Obit

Raised by cats,
she nevertheless
passed for human
most days, imperfectly,
making black marks on
paper where some saw
meaning, not meaning
muddy paws on the clean
sheet of what is.

To the Housesitter

It cannot feed itself. Please stay and be eaten
slowly in our stead. The cat is under the bed

and will not come to you.
Please feed him too.

Say if the rain

has stopped. (Outside the music umbrella is
the rain drumming down.)

Say if the cat scratched. (At the door. Your hand.
Needles from the tree. Needles in his paw.)

Is the sun rising so soon. Has the moon
begun to eat it. What an appetite

for fire. Say if you love. (Heat. Bed.
Good roast lamb. I am.)

Elementals

Only the top of the periodic chart
of possible marriages matters here.
Silicon beach, the iron in it
drawing lines in the sand, and ocean
H_2O with every spice in its soup.
A suit of water walking here
on her calcium rack rests
now in a tide pool under the hydrogen
sun, thinks
better of it with magnesium
brain which burns a blinding white
when a flame finds it.

*

The day of the dead falls in summer
this year, everyone's here, parents and sister

and friends, in this empty room, consuming the air.
My too many selves. The elderly cat. The books

and the marriage gone wrong. I have nothing
to say, and I say it. How like a tale

it might be told. Red hood or white cloak,
a passage from Janacek, a bearded

stranger one morning behind you suddenly
clutching, foreign lands, then suddenly

age, the sage of being alone, the
nowhere to go now.

*

When it's not the moon but the headlights of an SUV
in the dark, the squeal that says I'm turning into your street
and it does, the asphalt is gone, there's metal flashing and nowhere
to cross, Don't Walk, Don't Walk, that orange hand held high,
I stay on the stoop, yes here there are stoops, and you
are miles away. It stays. The minutes years. I age,
go gray. When the red taillights with third eye bright
as the devil pass, it's too late, I've seen the cloven
prints and breathed the sulphur in.

*

You can wipe the memory
from your phone, as if you'd never spoken.
Wipe your hard drive. Burn your poems.
Some government remembers
but you aren't a person of interest
or not so much. The word is still
in the river, caught
in the tide pools but cut
loose when the water rises.

*

The last question and then
the test is over. What will you do
when you're dead? Knit,
if you don't. There's no end to knitting.
Go on speaking into the silence
as if it were keepsake.
Take care of the cat,
the cat is still alive, and so
too a man, no rest
when the world ends.

Four Poems

The block is pink and lightest green with trees
and you are dying. What spring is this
and who will drink from it? Your fragile skin,
parchment I've written. At last
the body shudders and spasms
rest in peace. The woman across
the street fetches her baby into the sun
the violets sudden on the land
the dogs walking their humans.

*

So what if love
decays to an empty
cave where the walls weep?
Limestone, bed
rock, let the cathedral grow.

*

I nodded off and lost the poem. It was
Here in my throat and fingertips. Sleep is a glutton
I renounce. Even the cat strokes his cheek
On modern Greek. Sleep is a demon
I cast out, boar that it is.

*

Open window at last.
I've propped it with a dowel
and it won't slash down like the guillotine
it longs to be. The cat ecstatic,
a pyramid with a nose instead of that third
eye, greedy for knowledge at the peak.
Was it the longest winter? Ask him.
The one all habit and startle.

FACEBOOK: A GATHERING

FACEBOOK: A GATHERING

The moon is new and the sun is old.
The moon is full and the sun is empty,
eating its insides for light.
                    June 10, 2010

Someone has palmed the Ace of Hearts
from the base of the tower, and you are the shape
of the cards falling, until they have fallen.
                    November 3, 2011

One side of the card is blank. The other says life.
Every morning we draw and choose
to turn it over. Or not.
                    May 7, 2012

Thank you for the word, for the poem it encloses.
Thank you for bodies in motion, at rest. For faces
I trace with my fingers. For cats. For the web
of our writing. Thank you for families passing on sidewalks
after their feasts. For the whale atop the weathervane.
For solitude. For one soul walking in many bodies
everywhere singing. For breath. For breath.
                    November 22, 2012

Thirty Years With Anyone

Madness slow to unfurl. A blossom
Whose outer petals mean only color,
Hands with the light pulsing through them.

How slowly they give up their scent
One purl at a time, stop time
It's a film of frames however you

Walk, the sway when you
Walk hugged together on foreign streets
One tall and one long striding

One petal pressed in the book. They
Love you from balconies. It's the scent
Of mid-flower that intoxicates.

What's hidden in the bud takes years.
One can't speak, the other fears
What will be spoken once the

Rose is blown. On the bare stem
In the wind we know.
                          November 12, 2014

Oval Evening

Some gravity, two planets make the not quite circle.
The farther they move apart the more the orbit makes

Elegance lie in the graph. The planet burns and freezes
And we make no peace where peace would be easy.

Walk on the shore, see it shrinking. This place
Where we live is disappearing. Is there no love

For the poor, all those
Whose houses are sinking?
                          November 22, 2014

Sometimes I hear the click of the latch.
Not always. A room dissolves and I don't know how small the house
   is now
until the mansion of nightmares adds an annex.

Mostly clutter, the broken my back's
too old to bear away. I go to the kitchen to feed the cat from a box
and the room of mistakes, the closet of wrong

headed and hearted gossip in silence.
                    December 4, 2014

Tears
for the salt, Lot's wife
who dared to look back.
No god worth his water
would make a sin of that.
                    December 8, 2014

A Spell Against Christmas

I wish you joy, you who make light in the dark
with your trees. You make this hinterland

a city just for a moment. Just walk, electricity
pulses through imaginal reindeer,

who might fly were it not for wires, for children
if there were children, family

still alive or not gone missing. No spelling
out the word for longest night.
                    December 13, 2014

Out on the Cape

The dunes are thinking. Sand under wind under
moon, you can watch the crest build and break

Just as the ocean thinks, though the water
doesn't linger on conclusions, except in another

Ocean where it builds its plastic continent. What
could it be thinking about the trash? One more

Land to trouble its sleep and it wakes
from the nightmare with no it's not hopeless,

Sun is thinking on me now and nobody
knows where we're going.
December 15, 2014

Like a Lion

In a cage, the tiger who met me
Through the bars, his paws
The size of my head, his head
Oh his head. And the lion
The many lions too,
I'd rather die by them than by you.

The tiger placed his paws like flowers,
I swear, because there was glass. His face
Captive, wrong, so right as a tiger trapped.
He slammed full-body against the glass
And I'd still take him, whatever it costs.

The lions too. The females slinkies in the high grass,
The maned males reclining.
December 21, 2014

New Year

Already used. Musty.
It smells of what came before it.
If I could pick it up in my hands
I'd find my old wood stove
And feed the future into the past.
January 1, 2015

Like a thousand owls
The wind. Their Dies Irae
With a question mark,

Tonight? Tomorrow? Who
In the shaking houses and frigid
Nests, who who on the street

Is next. Who who
Will know what was taken
From the world when winter passes?
January 8, 2015

Comes the Propane

truck with its Jurassic rumble,
hose the saurian neck that spews
fuel and guzzles money. Dread
sound like the whisper
of cocaine the landlord's chosen
for you to live in, wrapped
in blankets in a box, frozen.
January 22, 2015

Just heard the wind yelp. The storm on its train
not due till midnight, give or take chaos.
              January 23, 2015

How did this moon get from window to window
so soon? So heavy and full
of itself it could not roll. Pearl of earth
are we the seed that troubled you?
                    May 5, 2015

Pomegranate
more wine than wine, deeper.
No wonder she followed
all the way down the red stairs
inside the white flesh.
                    August 19, 2015
                    (originally posted August 19, 2014)

Day of the Dead

The underworld, earth, and heaven, three
shelves of the altar. The middle world

on the middle shelf, how the gaze dwells
right in the center, the living who are dead to us

however we love them. Breathe copal, the resin
of amber, the preserver. I will be that dragonfly

perfect in your hand, a golden gem
held up to the light

anonymous in your pocket. The first shelf
all inheritance, a harrowing of what's not hell

but being born. In heaven as it deserves to be
Galway, Seamus, Flannery,

a crowded solitary party
where all have their Underwoods.
November 2, 2015
(originally posted November 2, 2014)

Like what you see? Become it, horizon palpable
On the sea, one shade off, enough to make you distinct.
The skull of a gull. The boat that needs to be taken
In, it's November, the ice

Is coming for your stern
Resolution and that warm
Motor you keep chugging.

Moon bright, a path to salt. Like what you see?
You wouldn't turn your back on a moon, you'd call
It right or what is left.
November 6, 2015
(originally posted November 6, 2014)

NOTES

"Mondrian's Forest" (p. 62): Many of Piet Mondrian's early paintings, including "Trees on the Gein," are Fauvist, representational in violent color. Equating the freedom of reason and science with spiritual freedom—partly in response to theosophy—he evolved the geometric style that made him famous. Kuan Yin is the Chinese Buddhist version of the Indian Avalokitesvara, goddess of compassion. [Author's note, *Little Apocalypse*]

"The Women on the Ward: Cassie" (p. 76): *Stelazine samba*: Many commonly-used antipsychotic drugs, including Stelazine and Thorazine, can cause "extrapyramidal effects," including involuntary movements and Parkinson's-like symptoms. [Author's note, *Little Apocalypse*]

"Six of One" (p. 86): *The terminator* is the astronomical term for the line dividing night from day on a planet's surface. [Author's note, *Little Apocalypse*]

"At the Synchrotron Lab" (p. 109): A synchrotron is a particle accelerator designed to force a collision of electrons and positrons; when matter and anti-matter meet, they destroy each other, releasing elementary particles. The Robert Wilson Laboratory at Cornell University, where this poem is set, discovered the "top" or "truth" quark. [Author's note, *Little Apocalypse*]

"The Dictionary of Improbable Speech" (pp. 78 & 101) is dedicated to the Crew, with thanks. [Author's note, *Little Apocalypse*]

SUBTERRANEAN MAPS: A POET'S CARTOGRAPHY

Wendy Battin

. . . we are such unconscious people. . .[1]
T.S. Eliot

The map is not the territory.[2]
A. Korzybski

1.

For all the years I lived in Boston, I had no car. My map of the greater city radiated from the black-on-white T's that marked the subway entrances: from Harvard and Kendall Squares, from Haymarket, from Government Center, the known world bloomed, the grid of streets filled in with shops and smog, corners where the balky *Don't Walk* signs had left me idling. The rest of my geography was underground. "How do I get to Newbury Street?" yelled a tourist, panicked in the mayhem of Storrow Drive. I couldn't help.

My map of literature is much the same. At fourteen I stumbled into a few poems by Ezra Pound; his London metro let me off in China, where I emerged into the sunlight of Lao-Tse and Li Po. And from Pound I followed the trail of dropped

First published in *Where We Stand: Women Poets on Literary Tradition*, ed. Sharon Bryan (New York: W.W. Norton, 1993), pp. 1-6.

names to *The Waste Land*, and on to Yeats and Stevens. I opened a paperback anthology to "Thirteen Ways of Looking at a Blackbird," and read,

> I do not know which to prefer,
> The beauty of inflections
> Or the beauty of innuendoes,
> The blackbird whistling
> Or just after.

It shocked me into silence, then into words: *I didn't know you could say that.* I went on writing my fourteen-year-old's doggerel, but I knew that somewhere on the other side of it I might find a way to *that*. Because language could do that, could break the loneliness of being conscious, could translate the buzz of perception into a call-and-response.

What Stevens gave me in that moment was the knowledge that I was real, that the sparks and shifts of my own mind happened in other minds, and that they had value in being shared. It was admission not to the private club of "literature," but to the human family.

My own map is larger now, starred by other shocks of recognition, by countless other writers who have shown me how to continue. But the tradition I write from is still an artifact of my loneliness; in the white noise of television, of the language made senseless by political lies and the lies of buying and selling, Shakespeare carries no more authority than Dickinson, than Han Shan or Akhmatova. I'm often angry that more women's voices have not been saved. I'm often amazed and grateful that any truthful voices have been saved at all.

If you bring me a cup of water in the desert, I will not ask whether you are male or female, whether you come from Paris or from Lagos. I could even conceive some nostalgia for the coherence of a central tradition, whether it wanted to admit me or not; but it would be too willful an invention, too chimerical and narrow to be convincing.

2.

Chimera:
—a mythological fire-breathing monster, commonly represented with a
lion's head, a goat's body, and a serpent's tail.
—Genetics: an organism composed of two or more genetically distinct
tissues, as an organism that is partly male and partly female, or an
artificially produced individual having tissues of several species.[3]

The only tradition I know is not a thing, but a process; not something we have, but something we do. My tradition as a poet is the sense I make of my being human, and the craft of that making; and, as "making sense" is a statement about order and value, i.e., about relationship, I make it from the sense that others have made. I make *myself*, continually, from the sense that other human beings have made. But for all my conjuring, the blank spaces on my map expand more rapidly than the map does. Maps from other cultures, from physics, linguistics, anthropology, from the homeless women I cook for and from the Taoist priest who teaches me martial arts, overlie my own and transform it. What else is it to be alive, in the chaos of the present?

And with whom will we commit our acts of tradition? I've recited a few stanzas of Yeats to a woman whose only address beyond "the street" is a psychiatric ward. Later she shouted to me from her corner, "Love is like the lion's tooth!" She knew what it meant. The shoppers scattered; Yeats, I think, would have been pleased.

3.

Whoever has approved this idea of order. . .will not find it preposterous
that the past should be altered by the present as much as the present is
directed by the past.
                    T.S. Eliot

My own historical sense includes the ebb and flow of feminist thought; I'm not disturbed that John Donne failed to recognize the full humanity of women, any more than I fault him for not including quantum mechanics in his world view. I am deeply disturbed when I encounter the same blindness in my contemporaries.

When I was an undergraduate in the early seventies, Sylvia Plath was the popular icon of the woman poet, and one day we heard that Anne Sexton had committed suicide. That night at a party, a male professor cornered me and asked, "Why do all you women poets kill yourselves?" I was twenty years old, awed by the real talent and knowledge of my teachers. I didn't say, "Because of people like you." I felt some of the anger and fear he might have intended me to feel; I felt even more the epistemological shock I've felt dealing with some schizophrenics, when a rift opens in their seemingly lucid speech and reveals the alien logic behind it.

Plath's mythographers, who claimed that she bartered her sanity for moments of genius, were spinning out a strand of Western literary tradition: Art at the price of Life, the Faust-haunted usury of spirit that admits of nothing that can't be traded or sold. I would not dispense with Goethe, who knew better; his Faust awakens from economics into *grace*, a word that even the most life-loathing monks had to learn from the body. But add the unconscious authority of that metaphor to the belief—equally unconscious?—that a woman has no right to poetry, and the resulting potion can be lethal.

But that's a use the living make of even the most eloquent dead; it's also more dangerously a use the dead—from their home in our underworld of hatreds and habits, inherited fears and loves—make of the living. Had that professor been momentarily hypnotized by some other theme, equally deep in his tradition—say, the artist as outsider—the news of a poet's death might have led him elsewhere. He might have chosen, if the same mood was on him, to threaten me as an artist rather than as a woman. That would have been, oddly, a more personal attack, and much less incongruous. The intellectual tradition we share includes detailed observations of primate social hierarchies and territorial drives, and even then I knew an aspiring alpha male when I saw one. We at least would have recognized each other as players on the same field, however unpleasant the game might be.

All the same, I beg his pardon for abstracting him into an icon in his turn—"nothing personal," I could tell him, to cover both my crime and my alibi, a sort of knee-jerk justice. He was a man having a bad day, perhaps; perhaps his bad days come less often now. And none of this map-making is of any use if the map forgets the territory, if the idea *human* abandons the changeable fumbling human. What Adrienne Rich once invoked as a "common language" must be, in the linear way of words, an intimate contract—I speak to you, you speak to me. Weave those numberless intimacies into a *shared* tradition and we have a Commons, that open field where the living can take up space and move freely, as the living must.

4.

> . . .*we know not why we go upstairs, or why we come down again, our most daily movements are like the passage of a ship on an unknown sea, and the sailors at the masthead ask, pointing their glasses to the horizon, Is there land or is there none? to which, if we are prophets, we make answer "Yes"; if we are truthful we say "No."* [4]

Because I know that my map is provisional, that I have pieced it together out of my own need, I am baffled when I encounter the guardians of any tradition who do not know that their maps are also partial, their historical sense equally sporadic. I have met scholars still unruffled by cybernetics in the nineties, who can base their lectures to the young on the assumption that the Cartesian duality, the divorce of mind from matter, is a law of nature; "secular" critics so xenophobic that they can attack a Zen-based work on "intellectual grounds," because it offends their unconscious Judaeo-Christian cosmology. When those premises go unchallenged, finally, I feel the same rifts opening, the same breach of trust among the living.

My own blind spots must be of similar magnitude. And so I end up embracing the chaos, the cultural relativism of maps stacking up, and fragments of maps. The early disorienting strangeness I felt, as a woman, as a member of the wrong class or caste, when I was confronted with the Monuments of Culture, has become for me, by now, an essential strangeness; I couldn't trust myself without it. I imagine any tradition that can hold both William Blake and Byron in a single thought can surely accommodate us as well. But it no longer surprises me when I'm taken for the barbarian at the gates—or for the cleaning lady at her subway stop. She's sometimes who I am.

NOTES

[1] All page references to Eliot from "Tradition and the Individual Talent," *Selected Prose of T. S. Eliot*, ed. Frank Kermode (New York: Harcourt Brace Jovanovich and Farrar, Straus & Giroux, 1975; originally published 1920), 37-47.

[2] Alfred Korzybski, *Science and Sanity* (New York: Science Press, 1941), 58.

[3] *Random House Dictionary of the English Language* (New York, 1969), 234.

[4] Virginia Woolf, *Orlando* (New York: Harcourt Brace Jovanovich, 1973), 78.

EARLY POEMS

Letter Toward a Successful Escape

Got your letter today. Thank you
for seeing Europe for me. The poem you
wrote on Yeats's grave
was terrible.
Why don't you go to Paris &
get laid?

Forget the British Museum, the manuscript
of Beowulf you
haven't read, and Stonehenge, my
druidical dreams.
Get drunk, get stoned, get fucked, get lost
in the Black Forest.

You saw my eyes
in a gift shop near Innisfree.
Don't marry them. Carry them
wrapped in gauze, an amulet against
the threat of sight. Lose them
at Monte Carlo; they'll take you wherever
you have no reason to go.
The Irish women have my
hair? Mine's cut like a nun's
now, strict with my face and drab
as old bath towels. There's no long
strand to pull you home.

You say that you're never alone, even
in London. You tell me I grow
in your mind, in your sleep.

I have no wish to be your tumor.
Have me removed. Like all
memory, I'm malignant.

Buy a guidebook for your Bible, and follow
its instructions to the teeth.
Learn to say "Your place or mine"
in seven languages. Cross
a border every day, and leave
your luggage in the station. Leave

the stationery in a hotel
drawer. The past is a cornered rat,
fighting these words.

The Time Warp

You've been here so often it feels like
the hospital.

It's only the hum
of the walls' breath, just
the carpet
sparking its fur.

Your mind is leaking.
Your mind is leaking.
It oozes around you, new chrysalis, old
transformation.

And the time warp, yes;
the night folds you up in its
chainmail gloves.

Scat on the Observable Universe

1.

It's portable,
electric.

Every morning it tails itself
to morning, &
hasn't scored
yet.

2.

Déjà vu is the basis of all
perception: the Irish
setter back with the
stick
for the ninety-sixth
time, or Congress.

I paint
a mountain on my
mirror, solid &
seen.

3.

I take the
curvature of space
as an act of

faith, since I'm balanced on
the lip.
We ask ourselves
where is the leak? &
what did you hide
in that black hole?

We take up
flag-pole-sitting on a March
day, solid &
seen.

Maya on Cape Cod

The patient woman turns to earth;
the screaming woman drowns in air.

She will learn the elements
one by one, the first being water.
Walking the beach daily
with her hair fanning
in the sun, or damp
and clasping her neck
when the sun refuses, she watches

everything that floats:
scallop boats, gulls
folded on the water
or unfolding; their cries
delay in the air, the ear, after
the birds wheel on. She tries
to hold her eyes to the white

line where the sky
and harbor tutor each other.

As if her days were programme music,
as if her instrument could be
tuned by the large hands that float
over her in sleep, lighting
like water, she waits;

she will be born
again, as Massachusetts Bay
in October. Everything that floats
is an apparition. She sees
much, holds nothing, and soon
the fleet will sail through her,
trading in fire, in earth, in air.

On Hearing of Suicides, and the Value of Chanting
for Julie Kane

Jasmine & speed, not good for the soul we
suspect. The speed goes always
upward, like the
Tao's improvidence, what if the
ladder's burning—
that flame in our hair's
ineluctable, &
we love the word. The word, the breath, the
existential leak in our common roof (howz it
            feel to be a lady poet?)
Only the elect can
kill themselves here. Planting four feet on the
ground reminds us our
ancestors sowed their acres with hen
teeth; on the farm, even the hens are speeding toward
Nirvana. As women we're made to
wonder where's our guilt in all this
enlightenment, when all these
fat-bellied buddhas will start giving birth
& give us peace.

She Awaits His Wrath

How to explain to him the long
fuchsia dress with
embroidery at your breast was your
two weeks' salary, and

the woman you sketched across
his sketch of you, and worst
of all your hair—your hair

swept from your sister's kitchen
floor, asleep in a brown
bag, waiting to grow
a new head. The night

will be hard, and full of hard faces.
It rattles its dice
in your bones' cups.

But if you could say your morning's eyes
saw death without rope or
gun, your prescriptions empty, then why not dance
joy that the corpse

walks, is warm and still
hot to his arms, why not
love this new woman who's

been out all day
saving lives?

October: A Love Poem

Three stragglers, Canada
geese headed north interlace
their lines of flight as if
to braid their intentions
together. Three? Your leisure, mine,
and another. Watch: the geese
locate their south, fly
out of their knot. The inlet
now reflects a world

quieter in its spectrum: oaks,
sky, the high cirrus washed
with a mute green;
as it should be, the water
that marries them visible.

In the Forest She Thinks of the Greater Body

Who sits in the tall
chairs of the woods?

Like hawks in the highest
storey of branches,
who saw what she saw in the green light?
The broad day in narrow
vertical swatches, in Dopplered
perspective?

Like krill through the strata
of ocean the sunlight
descended. Who felt what she felt
in her tree of nerves? Who thought
at the end of her spine that stalk
the cortical bloom?

Like lashes on the eye, limb upon limb
on the sky, past distinction.

Who sits in the tall
chairs of the wood,
in the woods' hall?

The Revolution

The last of the whooping cranes live
in the walls, hoarding everything
that disappears.
The temple cats
are gods again.
Terrible lizards, wooly
mammoths, Komodo dragons, the world's
one long medieval bestiary, and
how do we happen, speaking
no one's tongue.

We talk to our African violets,
our goldfish,
our children,
whatever can't walk out on us.
There are men who converse
in cuneiform—words
fall from their mouths and
shatter like mirrors. Our reflections
stick in our throats, fishbones
that haven't been fish.

Oh we have radar
bats never dream of.
At best we speak
like snakes, touching tongues.
Listen.
The whales chuckle quietly,
their playful language.

Cambridge, MA (Sept. 2006)

School photo (n.d.)

Mary McGovern Battin (n.d.)

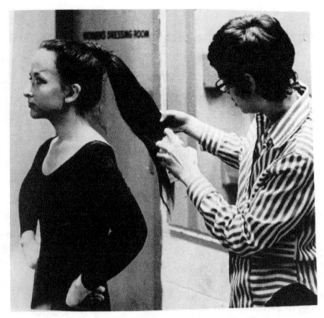

Gymnastics preparation (c. 1967)

Wilmington, DE (c. 1968)

FOR WENDY - CHRISTMAS '77   *Bill Zchalisz 1977*

Christmas 1977 (Provincetown?)

Brookline, MA (1983)

With Melinda Wagner (see "At Tanglewood")

Quebec City (July 2005)

Delphi, path up Parnassus (Nov. 1997)

Delphi, at Castalian Spring (Nov. 1997)

Mystic, CT (c. 2003)

Cape Breton (Aug. 2007)

With Fu, Mystic, CT (Nov. 2004)

Chania, Crete (May 2006)

Practice beside Aegina Harbor (Jan. 2007)

Kalyves, Crete, with USS Enterprise (May 2006)

THE LOVERS

Lucid Dreaming

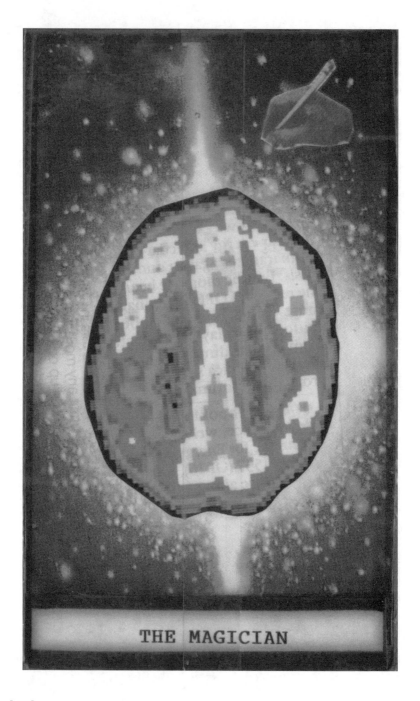

THE MAGICIAN

WENDY BATTIN:
PORTRAIT OF AN ARTIST AS A VERY YOUNG POET

Julie Kane

I'm not sure if I should damn my egocentric youth or praise it as Eden.
                         –Wendy, email to me dated 20 November 1997

I was terrified of eighteen-year-old Wendy Battin before she became my housemate and dear friend. She had entered Cornell University a year behind me in the early 1970s, one year younger but already well read in poetry and entirely sure of her opinions on any aspect of it. She was tiny, with a mass of long reddish-blond hair and freckles, and if you said anything dumb in workshop she would fix you with steely blue eyes behind wire-rimmed glasses, that silent stare more painful than any criticism voiced by anyone else.

Not only that, but she and I were editing rival literary magazines. Hers was *Rainy Day*, the official student organ. Mine was *Solstice*, an upstart zine founded by Mark Anderson, Gil Allen, Kate Dubina, and me out of frustration with the work *Rainy Day* was publishing before Wendy took over. But in actuality, during Wendy's reign we were both publishing each other and many of the same student poets.

It was the golden era of student poetry at Cornell, a harmonic convergence of sorts. Diane Ackerman, Gil Allen, Mark Anderson, Jim Bertolino, Sharon Dolin, Dan Fogel, Peter Fortunato, Cecil Giscombe, Rich Jörgenson, John Latta, Ken McClane, Stephen Tapscott, and Ross Tharaud were just some of the other student poets then, and the undergrads were as strong as the grad students. Judy Sue Epstein was back in Ithaca after fleeing the Iowa Writers Workshop, and Lynn Shoemaker was running the printing press at Ithaca House. Every Thursday afternoon in the Temple of Zeus coffeehouse in the basement of the English building, we would all get up and read our new poems to a packed audience including faculty members Archie Ammons, Bill Matthews, Bob Morgan, Billy Joe Harris, and cranky old Baxter Hathaway, the founder of Cornell's creative writing program.

So, I was somewhat apprehensive when Wendy asked me to be her housemate beginning in the fall of 1973, my senior year and her junior one. 206 Dryden Court was a ramshackle three-story Victorian tucked down an alley behind Johnny's Big Red Grill in Collegetown. Wendy and five other would-be tenants needed two more people to fill the bedrooms and split the rent, so Kate Dubina and I went to look at the place. The only two bedrooms not yet claimed were on the first floor, off a grimy kitchen with graffiti-covered walls. Someone had taped a map of the world over some of the writing, prompting these lines by Wendy: "Greenland is swollen / with latitude, & nothing / is sized right but New York" ("Perspectives: the mandatory poem"). Kate was going to be living with her boyfriend that year: she needed the address only for parent purposes. I imagined how noisy it would be trying to sleep with so many housemates partying late in the kitchen and clanging pots and pans in the morning. The rent was cheap. I signed the lease.

It only took one night of staying up late drinking and talking in Wendy's room for us to become fast friends and each other's first reader for new poems. Not only were we both passionate about poetry and "Women's Lib," as we then called it, but also, we had both been raised Irish Catholic in families with working-class roots. Wendy was from Wilmington, Delaware—a place she hated. I learned that she had been born twelve years after her only sibling, when her parents were in their mid-forties—a surprise (and not entirely welcome) pregnancy. Nobody in the family had been to college before Wendy. Harry and Mary Battin worked as clerks for an automobile dealer, and Wendy's big sister Ginny (already married, with two children Wendy adored) was an interior decorator. Into the Battins' devoutly religious lives Wendy dropped like an alien life-form: burning incense in her attic bedroom, embracing Buddhism and Druidism and shamanism, and scoring at genius level on standardized tests. In her ninth-grade yearbook, under "Ambition," Wendy put "poet."

We would have been drinking Old Milwaukee beer that night, the only brand we could afford, and chain-smoking red Marlboros, Wendy's hands trembling as she lit them. Her bedroom had a mattress on the floor and a solid wall of books. How had she amassed so many books, so young? Van Morrison's "Moondance," her favorite song, would have been playing over and over on her cheap stereo system, and if her cat Minnaloushe did not bite me that first night, he was just resting up for future attacks. The little beast had been named for the cat in Yeats's poem "The Cat and the Moon."

From that night on, whenever one of us finished writing a new poem, we would rip it out of the typewriter roller and charge upstairs (me) or downstairs (Wendy) to show it to the other. We talked poetry for hours on end and traded new poetry books back and forth ($2.95 in paperback at the Campus Store). Once, dissecting the latest Yale Younger Poets Prize collection, we counted on our fingers how many years we each had left to win it, the age cutoff being forty. Wendy lorded it over me that she had one more year of eligibility than I did.

Unconsciously, we began to influence each other's poetic styles. Wendy's poems took an uncharacteristic confessional turn, most memorably in "Letter Toward a Successful Escape." Her boyfriend the year before had been a tall, dark, and handsome engineering major who worshipped her. But the poor fellow was clueless about poetry, and poetry was the core of Wendy's being. Thinking to impress her, he had made a pilgrimage to Yeats's grave over the summer. Wendy was not impressed: "The poem you / wrote on Yeats' grave / was terrible. / Why don't you go to Paris & / get laid?" She broke up with him at the start of that fall semester and simultaneously chopped off all of her beautiful hair, as if she had taken vows of poetry: "The Irish women have my / hair? Mine's cut like a nun's / now, strict with my face and drab / as old bath towels." Meanwhile, my poems grew skinnier, like Wendy's, and they began pondering the mind-body connection, her constant theme.

Wendy had been a gymnastics champion and modern dancer in high school, and she would become a yoga instructor later in life. While others viewed ideas as abstractions, Wendy could not forget that the human body was the root of all perception and thought. Sometimes body seemed the master of mind: "Walking head down / against snow, the once / daily reminder that the body / does its thinking for you" ("Poet"). At other times, body was that Yeatsian dying animal we're all fastened to: "When we leave our bodies the din / will be /disgraceful" ("The Society of Astral Projectionists (SOAP) Papers"). Most often, though, body and mind coexisted in uneasy tension: "Poised on the spine (a / whiplash antenna), the / brain" ("Dancer's Bones"). Throughout that year, she was working on a long poetic sequence titled "Dancer's Bones." She believed from absorbing Eliot's *Waste Land* and Pound's *Cantos* that the long sequence was a litmus test of poetic greatness. And "Dancer's Bones" was nothing if not ambitious, weaving together themes of Cartesian dualism, feminism, the nature of the universe (she was enrolled in Carl Sagan's Intro to Astronomy course), and the unifying metaphor of the dance. But she tore up draft after draft, never satisfied with it, and to my knowledge, she never published it. One draft version in purple mimeograph ink, five pages long, survives among the papers I saved from our workshop with Bob Morgan.

Whenever Wendy had a few extra dollars, she would round up me and her other best woman friend, Jacquie Clark, to splurge on cheeseburgers and chocolate malteds at a Collegetown diner. Jacquie and I were both tall and, walking between us on the way there, Wendy would lament how she envied us our height. But there was nothing envious about her; nobody was a bigger cheerleader for her friends' successes. Jacquie was a modern dancer, and Wendy would praise her talent to me endlessly, behind Jacquie's back. She was proud that her two best friends were both creative artists. The year after I graduated, she would befriend Deb Auer from our poetry workshops, who went on to become a professional jazz singer.

Our evenings were usually spent in the Royal Palms Tavern, which was right across the street from Johnny's Big Red Grill. To the left as you walked in, under one of those wall murals with dogs in human clothes playing poker, was a long wooden picnic table where the poets sat. Stay in your room studying, or walk right out your door and across the street to sparkling literary conversation and dollar pitchers of beer? Even when it was snowing or sleeting, it wasn't much of a choice. That year our table was joined by Gerard Wimberly, who had just transferred to Cornell from LSU. Gerard affected silk scarves, paisley shirts, and corduroy pants tucked into Frye western boots; so of course, Wendy nicknamed him "Puss in Boots," and it stuck. We would drink and drink and drink until nobody had a dollar left for the next pitcher. Though we had a dollar deposit on the glass pitcher itself, returnable once we turned it back in, we could never figure out how to convert that last dollar to liquid gold.

"We have to get back to the music!" Wendy would shout over the din, at the height of our drunken poetry debates. That was her mantra. Like her idol Yeats, she wrote for the ear and not the eye.

We were both drinking way too much: "A hangover and a cold, after / much beer, long dancing, and one / decisive passing out" ("Perspectives: the mandatory poem"). But Wendy was not just drinking. She had a theory that junk piled up in the brain like trash on a sidewalk, and that she had to drop acid or nibble psychedelic mushrooms every so often to clear it all out. But she didn't always seem to come back whole from those mind-sweepings. By the spring of that year, she was cutting most of her classes except for workshop. And she made a halfhearted attempt to slash one wrist with a razor, calling to me from the landing between the first and second floors, then collapsing dramatically down the stairs when I emerged from my room. We got her admitted to the tiny psych unit at Cornell's Sage Clinic. The next morning, she phoned me with a list of things she needed, and I made the trek downhill to Sage with her nightgown, hairbrush, toothbrush, and poetry journal. It would not be the last time I made that journey with her personal things. As everyone who has ever loved Wendy knows, she lived in the shadow of depression.

She was lonely for a boyfriend after breaking up with Postcard Guy. Though she attracted men, she was picky: she was not willing to settle for a relationship without an intellectual or creative bond. There were a couple of one-night stands, which she invariably regretted:

"Waking up underwater; / in a busy intersection; / one more strange bed. / The body beside you / heaves / like a beached whale" ("The Pick-Up"). Then toward the end of that spring semester, her knight rode into town. Or rather, hitched.

Jess Roberts had drifted to Ithaca from somewhere in the Midwest where he was wanted for back child support, though we didn't know that yet. He was crashing with some friends who had a farm outside of town. Jess was easygoing, smiling, perpetually stoned, with a halo of shoulder-length blond curls. He wore the same outfit every day: a pair of overalls with no shirt underneath, so that if you got close enough to peek down one side you could see that he never wore any underwear, either. That must have saved him some time shucking off his clothes, which he seemed to do often, as the door to Wendy's room was often shut now, the floor mattress thumping.

"Streaking," in which a naked person dashes through some public event, was a strange and short-lived fad that year. During the televised Academy Awards show in early April, as David Niven was introducing Elizabeth Taylor, a naked guy had streaked across the stage flashing a peace sign. That is what prompted a wealthy couple in Ithaca to decide it would be funny to have their next party streaked. They enlisted Jess, who then tried to pitch me and Wendy to join him. We would get ten dollars each (Ten pitchers of beer! Twenty packs of Marlboros!) plus all the gourmet party food and alcohol we could consume, for a couple of minutes of "work." Sadly, my boyfriend at the time nixed my participation. But Wendy did it and enjoyed the hell out of it.

Jess was working odd jobs as a carpenter, but what Wendy truly loved about him was that he carved small wooden sculptures on the side. She immortalized one of them in a poem: "This sculpture sculpts / the hand holding it . . ." ("The Carved Bird, Unfinished"). Jess was a creative artist, like her, and that trumped being an engineering major with a bright material future. We all liked him, and we liked that he made Wendy happy.

Well, except for one more incident that spring: she swallowed a bottle of aspirin. Jess found her and phoned for help, and six cops rushed up the stairs carrying a stretcher and an oxygen mask. She got her stomach pumped and was OK afterward. I couldn't help wondering if she were just testing Jess, to see if he'd stick with her at her worst. At times, Wendy was even able to joke about her attempts at self-harm: "Monkey sells wristwatches . . . / Their wide bands hide / the scars on our wrists" ("How to Frame Nightmares"); and "You've been here so often it feels like / the hospital" ("The Time Warp"). But it was not very funny for her friends, who didn't know how to help her or save her.

I graduated in June and entered Boston University's creative writing M.A. program that fall. Wendy and Jess came to visit me soon after. She was entranced by the sea creatures in the New England Aquarium—we could hardly get her to leave at closing time. I took her to see the classroom where Robert Lowell had taught Plath and Sexton. Lowell was the golden boy of American poetry then, widely considered the country's greatest living poet, but Wendy was not buying it. She suggested that we launch a campaign to exorcise Lowell's ghost from Boston: arm ourselves with sledgehammers and go around smashing the Colonel Shaw statue on Boston Common, a couple of fish tanks at the Aquarium, some windows at 91 Revere Street. As it turned out, though, we didn't have to: Lowell's star would dim and his friend Elizabeth Bishop's rise without any criminal mischief on our part.

I saw a lot of Wendy that year, even though we were three hundred miles apart and carless, because I had started dating Puss in Boots, who like Wendy was a year behind me at Cornell. (When I phoned Wendy at home in Delaware over the Christmas break to tell her the romantic news, she was out but her mother kept me on the line complaining that Minnaloushe had smashed a set of cordial glasses.) Wendy was renting a house in Collegetown with a back balcony that hung—I am not kidding—directly over Cascadilla Gorge, a sheer plummet down hundreds of feet to rushing water and jagged rocks. Baxter Hathaway was her landlord. That house must have had some serious foundation issues.

One night we were having an impromptu party in Wendy's living room, made more festive than usual by the presence of an expensive bottle of scotch. Our poet friend John Latta had filched it from another party earlier that evening by flipping off the kitchen light switch as we were getting ready to leave, shoving it under his parka, and then flipping the lights back on again. Back at the gorge apartment, Wendy shyly held out a new poem for me to read. It was "On Hearing of Suicides, and the Value of Chanting," an acrostic that spelled out my name with the first letter of every other line. The suicide that had prompted the poem was that of Anne Sexton, our idol and my dear teacher at B.U. The poem refers to our shared Irishness ("our / ancestors sowed their acres with hen / teeth"), our bond as young women poets in a male-dominated environment ("howz it / feel to be a lady poet?"), and, best of all, our kindred heads of hair ("that flame in our hair's / ineluctable, & / we love the word"). Wendy would publish it in the final issue of *Granite* the following year.

She and Jess took a trip out west to look at MFA schools over the Christmas break. She phoned me from California, saying she hated it there and the visit with Jim Bertolino and his wife in Cincinnati had been strained, but she liked Tucson, where Richard Shelton had promised her a teaching assistantship. That summer I moved back to Ithaca for three months before starting a writing residency at Phillips Exeter Academy in September. Jess, suntanned in his loose-hanging farmer's overalls, kept me and Gerard supplied with vegetables he'd grown on the farm. Wendy was happy, excited about the future, and we two couples got together often.

•

She and I kept writing to each other and enclosing new poems as she went off to Arizona, then dropped out, then moved to Provincetown, Cape Cod, for a Fine Arts Work Center residency. It got renewed for a second year after she spent a summer driving dune-buggy tours. In one alarming letter from that period, she claimed to have destroyed her early poems. She was adopting the middle name "Tyg," she said—for Blake's Tyger? She had always loathed the name "Wendy," associating it with *Peter Pan*.

Then she went out west to try for an MFA again, this time at the University of Washington, and we lost track of each other. With the dawn of the Internet and email, we reconnected. Over the years, we made several attempts to get together when we were in the same city or region, but it never seemed to work out. At AWP in Portland in 1997, pre-cell phones, our hotels would not connect our calls. (I had brought my boyfriend at the time, an ER physician, with me. Wendy had suggested beforehand that we meet for drinks, and I had responded that for old times' sake we ought to make it cheeseburgers and malteds. "In that case, I might well need your friend's medical aid," she messaged back.) In July of 2009, she was supposed to drive up from Mystic to see me in Boston, but she got into a fender-bender the day before, and she and the car were too shaken up to make it. We transitioned to Facebook and to sporadic posts and private messages; and it was on Facebook that I learned of her death.

She was one year younger, a head shorter, a junior to my senior, with a whole extra year of days dealt out to her in which to win the Yale Younger Poets Prize. How is it that the seashell I carry with me always, in my purse, is from the beach where I tossed a handful of her ashes into the sea?

•

It was an Eden, and I was with her there.

SEQUENCE AND DAILINESS

Stephen Tapscott

I think one of the largest themes in Wendy Battin's work, beginning in her first book, is one familiar to dancers and practitioners of yoga (Battin was both) and visual artists: the question of the relations among representation, performance, and time. The poet, the dancer, wants continuity, flow, accountability, grace, the perfect moment in its material Is-ness. And at the same time there are limits: the limits of how much a body can do, of time, of momentariness. A dance moves linearly through time. A dancer's body ages. Can one performance be the "dance," or only an instance of it? A photographer wants to make a single image that "stops time," but she knows that time does not stop. Can she make an image of the passing of time? The theme will require an art that can both register intermediate closures and register or embody change.

One great discovery of Battin's first book is the format of the linked lyric sequence. It's a flexible form, one that was revived recently enough for us to recognize models. Around the time of the book, Robert Penn Warren's *Audubon: A Vision* (1969) and Galway Kinnell's *The Book of Nightmares* (1971) were fiercely influential. The form permits a linear momentum (even an implied narrative) but with occasions for lyrical extrapolations, discontinuities, diversions, intermittent closures. Because the Is-ness of the world or of its story cannot be static, we have to account for changes, motion, even error and irony in the paths of possibility . . . and yet we do have a sense, at times, of a hard-won or ecstatic provisional truth. This combination of intermediate stopping point and longer arc of change is the essence of the lyric sequence, and Battin's discovery of the format, and her mastery of its suggestiveness, underlie the best poems in both her books, it seems to me. The form allows several metaphorical systems to coexist in the poem at the same time, or in sequence at least (a recurrent moral moment in Battin's poems, especially in *Little Apocalypse*), or even several narratives to be conducted at the same time. The world is various.

The lyrical sequence is an important discovery—for Battin and also for her poems as metonymies of the mandate of a generation of poets who were working through a transition: from post-Confessional self-revelation to ... well, something new that could honor the discoveries of political and psychological selfhood while admitting other influences, other modalities, other needs. In part, the lyric sequence permitted the introduction of abstraction—sometimes provisional, sometimes intermittent—while not committing the whole lyric to totalizing narratives. I think of the ways that A.R. Ammons and Robert Morgan, for instance, use scientific vocabularies and philosophical abstractions in the interest of their narratives of dailiness, of life-in-the-mind . . . and I remember that Ammons and Morgan were at Cornell during Battin's undergraduate years there. Were they her teachers? They were certainly the dominant aesthetic models on the scene—powerful poets and empathic, generous mentors, capacious imaginations. I suspect a line of influence there, just as I sense a lot of Emily Dickinson in Battin's work. Read the Dickinson fascicles, or read Ammons' *Snow Poems* (1977), and a different relation to abstraction emerges: it's threaded through the dailiness.

This relation between dailiness and abstraction, between narrative and signification, between lyric and science, is part of the dynamic that Wendy Battin's first book boldly negotiates. By the time of the second, Battin has harnessed the power of the lyric sequence, with its capacity for implied narrative and wide-ranging diction. I'm interested in how the first book works towards the supple sequencing of the title poem, at the end of the book. Here, at the conclusion of that sequence, she returns literally to the issues that poems like "Christina Falls" (the first poem in the book) had raised, as they thought about eroding historicity and the events of our lives: how we rely on memories, and stories, and maps, and names, to orient us, while acknowledging that those orientations themselves change. They don't lie to us, but they aren't permanent either, any more than human relationships are permanent, or the wisdom of dreams is. The final sequences of *In the Solar Wind* even include an element of self-consciousness, as if the poet is aware also of the reader, watching her "pace" back and forth (an image of poetic enjambment? Or is she the anxious sleepless woman in the poem's implied narrative?), with the knowledge that representations change, that people and memories change, that our names are (as Keats said) written in water. Watch how these issues work themselves out, maturely and confidently and satisfyingly, in the final sections of the final poem of *In the Solar Wind:*

> You are here, listening,
> watching me pace.
> You will stay to find out
> what happens, what happens.
> You will want to know why.
>
> I can tell you: the story goes on
> and leaves us behind.
> The teller forgets,
> and the story finds a new tongue, new breath
> to ride on.
> The listener turns in his sleep
> and then he is gone.
>
> *
>
> She is sleeping. She is standing
> in the next room and picks up
> the scent of almonds.
>
> She has just emerged from the woods
> and follows
> the needle path down to the lake
>
> where she will
> stop to see her face
> in the surface of the water.

THE MOUNTAIN'S VOICE

Pamela Alexander

Wendy Battin is a poet who puts pressure on language until it gives. And what it gives—that present she has arranged for herself and her reader—she unwraps with utmost care. Winner of the Richard Snyder Memorial Prize, her book *Little Apocalypse* is more about seeing than about the self who sees. It is a portrait of perception itself, a mind giving itself away.

Among the aphoristic sections of the *ars poetica* of the book, "Sense, Sensed," is one that comments on the stance of the seer, the "I" who is fully present and yet able to stay out of her own way:

> I work to be changed,
> or someone like an I,
> though hardly enough to interrupt a mirror.

The second line is crucial. The "I" here is an instrument of language and observation, not an autobiographical speaker—a relatively rare stance that gives the poems plenty of room to play. Another excerpt from the same poem:

This essay was first published as "A Measure of Measures: Poetry and Poetics" (review of *Little Apocalypse*), *The Boston Book Review*, Volume 4, Issue 6, July / August 1997.

The poet bends in language like
a rose in its bud vase,
green stroke of its stem alive and

broken at the water line,
shifted away from itself at the point
where water baffles the light.

The exact and exacting choice of "baffles" is just the sort of playful illumination that characterizes the book. And "shifted away from itself" resounds with metaphor: self is displaced slightly by not-self at the point at which the poet disappears into language.

A poet who works out of self in this sense is likely to be attracted to the borders and boundaries of consciousness, such as the altered states of sleep and waking, of memory and the many forms forgetting takes, of language and the letting go and reinventing of it. The first poem in the book, "Anamnesis," takes on the paradoxical state of the forgetting of forgetting, and draws us into this lovely passage:

Alpha calm, beta, dreamy delta, theta:
the mind wanders from window to window, peering out.
That was a Monarch or a Viceroy, not a ragged leaf.
The gust lofted its deep V straight,

as if up a shaft; how does its startled insect brain
spark, filter, make geometry,
when the world moves it?

And, by extension, how does a startled human brain spark and filter?—a brain that has done the work of a poet, which is to go out of its way to be startled, not to take for granted the extraordinary fact of being alive to ask such a question. *Little*

Apocalypse can be imagined as a series of illustrations by way of an answer.

> Someone I loved
> and spoke to in all my tongues,
> 　　　　　who listens now
> 　　　　　though nothing is left inside
> but the hearing.
> Though who it was had burned away.
> And I must call up the others,
> 　　　　　the loves I can name
> 　　　　　to be silenced.

As in her first book, the National Poetry Series winner *In the Solar Wind*, Battin delights in everything—the truth quark and Tai Chi, etymology and echolocation, seasonal variation in chickadee vocalization and the disordered order of minds on a psychiatric ward. Eclectic subjects make for lively reading, even if they do present difficulties for critics characterizing the book in excerpts. Battin was surely aware of her imagination's wide engagement: "Who said // the conscious mind is like a flashlight? Whatever / it looks at is bright." Whatever *Little Apocalypse* looks at is also intensely human; while this poet may be uninterested in autobiography, she is not distant. "Drosophila," for example, begins in a classroom where

> fifteen-year-olds with their seed
> swarming in their ovaries and balls
> study the long Mendelian
>
> lottery: the politics of chromosomes,
> of dominance and
> the recessives banding together
>
> to be heard.

It ends with the girl who smuggles fruit salad from the cafeteria for some extracurricular breeding, who wishes for the lyrical mutation—not the ordinary red or white, but "jade eyes / that look back in recognition." Held in the human gaze of these poems, the natural world looks back with recognition and intelligence. It has been "sensed"—as in the poem "Sense, Sensed":

The fox in the field is a standing wave,
a graph of attention.
Then he breaks for cover. The wave snaps flat
into red direction.

Tone, like content, ranges widely. Battin is not unwilling to entertain some tongue-in-cheek antics, as in the four poems titled "*From* The Dictionary of Improbable Speech." Or as in the delightful "Hallowing All, Chris Smart," a parody of the famous poem "Jubilate Agni" and a (possibly eponymous) paean to the bat. More subtly, a humor arising from affection is imbedded in the line breaks of "Six of One," from the exquisite sequence "Lucid Dreaming":

Six of One,

half a dozen of the almond biscotti, the cappuccino
steaming. Love demands good food and some small

crime against the sensible. It says this morning
we are not poor, this morning is a cul-de-sac

off the main drag.

When one has netted a butterfly the proper technique is to lay the net on the ground with one fold in it, a sufficient barrier to hold but not damage the captive. Meanwhile the lepidopterist hunts farther, or consults her field guide, or eats lunch. I discovered the one-fold technique at age eight, as my high-schooler sister swished her way through bushes with the determination of someone with a science project due the next day. One of her nets lay on the grass beside me; bored, I picked it up, planning to do some copycat swishing myself. A butterfly made its escape past my startled face.

Wendy Battin's poems are nets that retain the proper fold. The rare, winged creature will not escape; it is alive and available for our inspection. It is tempting to suggest that Battin's lifelong connection to science is the source of her non-self speaker and of the care implicit in the protocol of her lines. But other interests of hers can be seen to bear—the discipline of yoga, the contained exuberance of dance. In any case, her agile poetry exhibits the quality shared by scientists and artists, the urge to explore, as witnessed by the varied subject matter with which this book concerns itself. The poems themselves are process—they proceed down the page in a way that is surprising but inevitable. Here are the tracks of a tuned consciousness, an essential poetic imagination.

With the flexibility of a cat and the unnerving accuracy-on-the-wing of a bat, these poems of language-as-perception accumulate into an extraordinary book. That a poet can be in love with the world and the things of it (coelacanth, relativity, you, almond biscotti, Mondrian) and yet able to stand slightly aside from them, to see them with luminous newness, is one of the primary virtues of *Little Apocalypse*. "Poets have voices the way mountains have hermits," Battin says. Her voices are full of light.

THE PHYSICS OF LOSS:
WENDY BATTIN'S "AT THE SYNCHROTRON LAB"

Sharon Bryan

One of poetry's central powers is to juxtapose and reveal connections between apparently disparate things: Emily Dickinson's buzzing fly with the moment of a person's death; Albert Goldbarth's nimble steps from laptops to werewolves to silent movies to shooting stars to Fallopian tubes in just two stanzas of a poem; Terrance Hayes's rocketing from pompoms and school mascots to bananas to Caligula, butterflies, goldfish, and pumpkin pompadours in a single sonnet. Sparks shoot across the gaps as one thing connects to another.

Wendy Battin's poems also touch on a wide range of subject matter: paintings, mythology, physics, yoga, love, grief, fruitflies, frogs, Tarot, and particle accelerators, among others. But as I've been re-reading her poems I've realized that she is not making connections as she goes, but that the poems start from the assumption that these things are all part of one reality to begin with. Their universe is a seamless whole, not a fragmented one. The poems don't set out to dazzle us with their discoveries or convince us of similarities between one thing and another. Instead, they speak out of and reveal a mind that sees everything as of a piece.

One of the poems that most brought this home to me is the last poem in her second and last book, *Little Apocalypse,* published by Ashland Poetry Press in 1997. "At the Synchrotron Lab" is forty lines long, ten quatrains. The very first line establishes a layered reality:

> In the sunlight of the upper world, the bookkeepers sit,
> and the secretaries, over mugs of coffee—
> mugs with red hearts or Japanese
> irises on their long stalks, mobius brushstrokes.

It's that "upper world" that gives me a little frisson of more to come: here's the very ordinary office, with bookkeepers and secretaries, but don't mistake it for the whole picture. The next stanza moves in to focus on one of the secretaries:

> She is plump, twenty-three. They are planning her wedding.
> the bridesmaids in turquoise. No, coral. The flowers.
> The professor asks her type, and she does:
> lambdas, omegas, the beta a B on its rocking tail.

Here again, it's almost ordinary, except that slightly awkward third line, which summons an entire little dance between the professor, who seems to be flirting, and the secretary's willful misunderstanding. She might not follow the research she's typing beyond its appearance, but she has much better social skills than the professor does. She's also adept at doing more than one thing at a time:

> Her skill is so sharp in her fingers she thinks
> *the new house   the man's bed   the money   the child*
> *the next step*   and makes no mistake.
> Downstairs they're arguing voltage and money,

In that fourth line we get our first glimpse of what lies below this upper world: "voltage and money." But there's so much more:

> and the quarks in their colors and flavors: *up, down,*
> *charm, strange, truth, and beauty,* real
> as love or numbers, true
> as a fable. Like this one: a woman walks over the earth

Suddenly the poem has sped up—accelerated—in every way. The first two stanzas end with periods, the third ends with a comma, and this one ends with no punctuation at all. But there's a lot to take in here before we rush into the next stanza. Quarks are a type of elementary particle and a fundamental constituent of matter. They were first proposed independently in 1964 by the physicists Murray Gell-Mann and George Zweig. Zweig wanted to call his model the "ace," but Gell-Mann took the much more poetic "quark" from a passage in James Joyce's *Finnegan's Wake*:

> — Three quarks for Muster Mark!
> Sure he hasn't got much of a bark
> And sure any he has it's all beside the mark.

Battin knows all this, and trusts us to do our homework if we don't. She isn't explaining the world she lives in, she's simply showing us around. She revels in the whimsical names for different quarks, then describes them as "real / as love or numbers." She couldn't be clearer: everything is equally real, what we see and what we can imagine. How different is a physicist's vision from a poet's? They both glimpse shadowy shapes, and both try to name them, to put their visions into words. But then there's one more twist in the stanza: "true / as a fable, a woman walks over the earth." So fables too are true, as true as quarks and love and numbers. I follow as the "woman walks over the earth"

with a lamp, looking for One. She looks in the sky
as it blues and darkens. She looks in the whorl of a geode,
she looks in the satin ear of a shell,
in a mole's stunned eye, in the alleys of the capital,

This woman isn't looking for "the One," as the secretary
might be, and despite the lamp I don't think she's searching for
one honest man (though as soon as I say that I think of a sense
of loss and betrayal in the book's first poem, "Anamnesis," the
return of memories we'd like to forget). Instead, I think first—
because I know that Battin taught and practiced it—of yoga. *Yoga*
comes from a word meaning "yoking," as oxen, so they can work
together. The goal in yoga is to unite the parts of the mind. And
then, because I know of Battin's fascination with metaphysics as
well as physics, I think of Plotinus and Neoplatonism. Plotinus
(b. 204 C. E.) based his work on his reading of Plato to construct
a cosmology based on three principles: the One, the Intelligence,
and the Soul—something that to a nonpractitioner sounds a little
like yoga's concepts of the external body, the internal soul, and
the mind that moves between them. No matter how many layers
are added they still seem to make one whole.

But of course the woman is still walking, and looking—at a
geode, a seashell, a mole's eye. And I realize these are all examples
of a Fibonacci series. It's a sequence of numbers that takes
three-dimensional form throughout nature, in branching trees,
artichoke leaves, pine cones, pineapples, cactus—the examples
are endless. The series begins with 0 or 1, and each subsequent
number is the sum of the two previous numbers: 1, 1, 2, 3, 5, 8, 13,
21, 34, 55 .... Though they were introduced to western thinking in
the 13th century by Fibonacci, I discover that they were actually
first mentioned in the 2nd century B.C.E. by someone named
Pingala, as he was analyzing patterns of . . . poetry. Of course.
And I know that Battin would have known that. And known that

the sequence of numbers also appears in Sanskrit poetry. As for the "alleys of the capital"? The Fibonacci series is also found in architecture. At this point, the woman seems to be looking for a place to begin (once this book is behind her), and a path to follow.

And, at last, we come to the synchrotron:

and she is unafraid. If she finds it, she can seek Two.
Here, under the field with its harsh cropped grass,
the magnets rest in their tunnel.
They are painted the primary colors of code, red, yellow,

blue, for they steer the invisible. Electrons shoot clockwise.
The positrons, their mirror image, double negatives,
fly widdershins into *annihilation*—
that is their word now, and the blade of their precision.

I can't help wondering: where is this being seen from? Is the speaker describing something she saw in person? In a book? I could imagine her visiting the secretaries, but was she actually allowed underground? Did she work there? Much of the time the poem seems to be spoken by a third-person narrator, but I know that in the next stanza an *I* appears and stays, so I imagine her discreet presence behind the whole poem. Only when I came to the notes at the end of the book did I find out that the synchrotron she's referring to is at Cornell University (the best-known one now is the Hadron particle accelerator in Switzerland). Which is where I first met Battin, and studied poetry with her, but did not even know about what lay under the "harsh cropped grass." That's one more measure to me of her x-ray like vision, her ability to see endless layers simultaneously. In the note, she describes the synchrotron as "a particle accelerator designed to force a collision of electrons and positrons; when matter and anti-matter meet, they destroy each other . . . . The Robert Wilson Laboratory, where this poem is set, discovered the 'top 'or 'truth' quark." Maybe this rhymes with "true / as a fable," and the woman looking for one honest man. Maybe underlying the image of the synchrotron are two people destroying each other. Again, I think back to the book's first poem, "Anamnesis": "Anamnesis, it's called, when forgetfulness is lost." Forgetting to forget, remembering despite yourself, the memory intruding suddenly, "the way a migraine can" or as "when I saw him angle a log in the fire, intent / on building strongly and well what was already burning."

Based on their electrical charges, electrons and positrons are indeed "mirror image[s], double negatives." Splitting the atom can lead to annihilation: "the state or act of being completely destroyed or obliterated," according to my dictionary, but so can other kinds of loss, "with the blades of their precision." And now we come to the book's oxymoronic title:

> The little apocalypse repeats and repeats. I can see it
> in the dials, in the needles swinging. The digits roll up
> in their windows. This lab
> is full of the paraphernalia of light—the spectroscope,
>
> oscilloscope, the meters and glassy lucite cable
> coiled on the workbench like a failed basket—
> to hold the flash that comes
> when the matter breaks open, and whatever the numbers
>
> say about the world. Is it only that the world
> is in the numbers, in the tracks through a cloud chamber?
> And in this probing: what I close
> my hand on, name, forget. Then want again.

No apocalypse is actually small in its impact, no matter how small its components: It's the end of something, a violence, "a large disastrous fire, an inferno," according to my dictionary, which offers this example of using it: "Most foresters agree that smaller controlled burns are essential to prevent a larger apocalypse." But sometimes those smaller burns get out of control—perhaps like the well-tended fire of the first poem in the book. There are all the warning signs of what's to come, in the dials, in the needles. I almost didn't look up the wonderful word *paraphernalia*, because I knew it meant something like "gear," "equipment," all the specifics she's describing. But why *that* word for it, which summons up a messy workshop more than a physics lab? And then I learned one more thing: it comes from a Greek word, *parápherna*—meaning "the separate real or personal property of a married woman that she can dispose of by will and sometimes according to common law during her life." I had thought I might have been reading too much into the poem, seeing things that weren't there, but as always Battin was way ahead of me. The poem began with secretaries fantasizing about a wedding. And there's that failed basket—meant to hold something. Is what happens to us written in numbers? How much is fate, and how much free will? In a cloud chamber, we can see the traces of matter, of what's otherwise invisible. Like our pasts, what we remember and forget. We try to take hold of something, however elusive, name it, forget it when we lose it. Because the woman wandering over the earth has brought us with her on the journey, we too can finally see all the layers she sees and feels. See them all at once, like overlays of the human body in an anatomy book, all the systems crucial. But this is an anatomy of what it is to be mortal in the universe, and at the heart of it all, the deepest level, is wanting. And letting go. And wanting again. No amount of knowledge or practice will change that: "The little apocalypse repeats." And now that we've seen it all so clearly, we too will keep forgetting to forget.

BETWEEN INTIMATION AND RECOGNITION

John Gordon

Wendy Battin's poetry is never, I think, obscure. On the contrary, it is written in a vein of unfussy precisionism, and what confused the first time around either always or almost falls into place on reconsideration. The reconsideration may sometimes require some thinking-through and checking-out. For instance, the "carnivorous" sphinx of her poem "The Women on the Ward" lit, for me, a very dim bulb, resolved by checking *Wikipedia*, which reminded me that if you got her riddle wrong the sphinx would eat you.

Most interesting poetry, I venture, occurs at a liminal midpoint of difficulty, situated somewhere between "The Charge of the Light Brigade" and "Altarwise by Owl Light." Battin's poetry specializes in borders, in their meetings, overlappings, and crossings, and one of them is between intimation and recognition. She is, in her way, a metaphysical poet. Samuel Johnson, in a generally hostile essay, did concede this about the original metaphysicals: "to write on their plan it was at least necessary to read and think." Add "read" to "write" and that is, often, us, negotiating her poetry. And, after all, consider the alternative, the alternative being material requiring no thinking whatsoever. It's not as if we were all of us suffering from a dearth.

The following is a list of annotations and commentaries, suggesting answers to a number of passages that puzzled me on first reading.

In the Solar Wind

"Christine Falls on the Road to Paradise." "Farewell-to-spring" and "mountain misery" are the names of regional wildflowers; the latter does indeed have five white petals, here recalling DaVinci's "Vitruvian Man," with its geometrically distributed head and limbs.

"Letters from Three Women." "When the letters bloom out of their envelopes / I think it must be spring": Letters come in envelopes and so do garden seeds, to be planted in spring. They can be ordered through the mail.

"The Lighthouse Has No Keeper." "a dolphin / clicks. Its word in the water / is 31 meters long": Dolphins issue clicks for echolocation. The length of time it takes for the echo to return establishes the distance—in this case, 31 meters—from the object to which the click was directed.

"Waking." "A slow sine wave into day, / surfacing from the aquarium": A sine wave is the kind displayed on an oscilloscope. Think of Kubrick's *2001* (Battin knew her science fiction) and, below, see the note for "Anamnesis." Here, the brain's wave pattern during the transition from sleep to waking. "The aquarium" is sleep, out of which we rise and shine, as if from underwater.

"Maya at Equinox." Charles Hartman informs me that "Maya was a character she invented to embody the Buddhist notion of the 'veil of illusion.'"

"Phlogiston." Briefly and a bit over-simply, the alchemist who thought up phlogiston was Johan Joachim Becher, to account for what was lost when fire consumed, for instance, wood. Joseph Priestley's discovery of oxygen, here at work burning up "dry juniper," supplanted it. Becher's theory involved revising the ancient doctrine of bodily humors, according to which macrocosmic fire corresponded to microcosmic blood, the "igneous humor" of this poem. Hence, "We breathe / juniper smoke, oxygen, / adding the gases to our blood." Probably a nod as well to Lavoisier, who extinguished a candle and then killed a mouse by depriving both of oxygen, and concluded by analogy that breathing delivered oxygen to the blood, where it was burned as fuel.

"Invention of the Phoenix." No coincidence that this title follows a poem set in Tucson; again, Battin's poems sometimes share wavelengths. That "The phoenix is false," that "we made it / from pieces of bird and the idea of fire" traces to a major premise of empirical philosophy (Locke, for instance)—that we cannot imagine something whose constituents we have not experienced. We can imagine a unicorn because, and only because, we already know what a horse is and what a horn is.

"In the Solar Wind." "To the molecules / every wall is a window": Well, no—but later on "we have chosen a world / that splinters and shifts, // from molecule to atom / to particle to quark," and, yes, that does make a kind of sense, familiar in Battin's poetry, where organic and atomistic, sand dune and sand, water and mist can be epistemologically interchangeable. Later, in the same poem, "the maps unfold in a small boy's hands" into state, county, planet, etc.: again, microcosms and macrocosms, by degrees, interchangeably. (But not necessarily reversibly: some younger readers may not remember the pre-Siri roadmaps that used to be stuffed into glove compartments—easily unfoldable, but trying to refold them, like trying to reverse the Big Bang, could be another story.)

Little Apocalypse

"Anamnesis." "Alpha calm, beta, dreamy delta, theta": four out of the five types of "brainwaves" of neural oscillation; delta is indeed the "dreamy" one. The fifth, gamma, never named here, would be the one in operation in the lines immediately following, discerning that a "Monarch or Viceroy" (the two are almost identical) perched outside the window is a butterfly, "not a ragged leaf," that in a gust of wind its wings fold up, collapsing their acute-angle V into a straight line.

"Creation Myths." "Why we lose our keys in the dark and hunt for them / under the streetlight": known as the "streetlight effect," a textbook example of observational bias. Based on an old joke: someone loses his keys in the park but looks for them under a streetlamp. Asked why, he answers, "Because this is where the light is."

"Coelacanth." Not a thing of beauty, but, still, an exemplary border-dweller: living fossil (long thought extinct), "related," says *Wikipedia*, "to lungfishes and tetrapods," anatomically as hybrid ("Dear monster") as any duckbilled platypus. "Estuarial" because in its amphibious heyday, about 400 million years ago, there was as yet no make-up-your-damn-mind *diktat* that "river be river and ocean, ocean."

"One." At the outset of a sequence tracking morning hours from one to seven a.m. (plus a "Coda," making eight, hence "the octave of his sleep," those being the eight hours recommended for sleepers), these words: "odd that this fulcrum rests / in the middle of darkness." Which is puzzling, because midnight, not one, is conventionally the fulcrum between night and morning. But the rest of the sequence makes it clear that the date is somewhere between March and October. So: Daylight Savings Time. Spring forward. Twelve becomes one, and one is an "odd" number.

"Seven." "the body's virtue is renewal. Cell after cell": The title is a clue to the tradition, otherwise uncited, that the body's cells renew every seven years. "Virtue," probably in the sense (*OED*, "virtue," 6A) of "superiority or excellence in a particular sphere"; compare Chaucer's "of which vertu engendred is the flour." Earlier, "the seven heavens, transparently stacked / like an archaeological dig into glassworks": envision a scale model of the Ptolemaic cosmos, seven concentric spheres of crystal, with a cutaway through which the amputated edge of each circumference appears to be a "stratum" "stacked" above or below the others. "The virtue of mercury is speed": As planet, Mercury's orbital speed exceeds that of the others; as god, Mercury the messenger was the swiftest; as element, mercury is in fact "rapid and silver," slithering electrically over any surface. Everything else Battin says about it is true too.

"Sense, Sensed." "The fox in the field is a standing wave, / a graph of attention. / Then he breaks for cover. The wave snaps flat / into red direction." "Standing wave": "a wave which oscillates in time but whose peak amplitude profile does not move in space." "Snaps flat" as in flatlining—the fox's headlong course, a straight line inscribed by a red point, its red self, racing toward its native home in the far, red end of the color spectrum. (The next gradation, infrared, would make it invisible, therefore safe.) Later, "the firewood that warms twice": chopping it and burning it.

"Like the Second Hand on a Very Slow Watch." March 1986, Halley's Comet. For various reasons it was a dud, "a faint scar of light." "Muybridge," juxtaposed with "Zeno": for the former, the question was whether a racing horse ever completely left the ground, for the latter, whether the racing Achilles ever completely made it to the finish line.

"Calling & Singing." Again, simply true: in mating season, a chickadee's call is two notes; later, it's what any bird watcher will tell you is its own name: "Chick-a-dee-dee-dee."

"Frog. Little Eden." To be precise, a tree frog, one with a religious turn of mind: the tree top is his second paradise (the first was his pond), as witness the fact that, against all visible laws of physics, water climbs up through the tree's "root-hairs"—trunk, branches, twigs—whenever he wills it. Probably a case of *post hoc ergo propter hoc*: I speculate that it's really the other way round, that frogs take to the trees after not before the sap starts rising … but so what? Miraculous either way. J. D. McClatchy is right about Battin's "deeply religious imagination."

"At Tanglewood." "ammonites": Tanglewood is in western Massachusetts, a region loaded with fossils, including ammonites—seashells, here dreaming back, Yeats-like, to the days when everything around was underwater. (Again, Battin's affinity for the amphibian.) The Tanglewood shed is commonly called a shell.

"Saguaro National Forest." "Caliche" is sedimentary, a dry crust formed from absconded oceans. The native saguaro cactus, drinking, through its tap root, "the water in the back of the desert's / mind," is an extreme equivalent of Tanglewood's ammonites.

"Mystic." "Better a museum": Mystic, Connecticut was once in the business of killing whales. Now it has a museum instead. Better.

"At the Synchrotron Lab." Out of my depth here, but "lambda," "omega," and "beta" all figure in the classification of atomic particles, and lower-case beta does have a "tail." (Evidently the typist's keyboard includes Greek letters.) "*Up, down, charm, strange, truth, beauty*" are all quark names, and "colors" and "flavors" also figure in quark terminology. I would bet that Battin lists "*truth, and beauty*," in that order, in homage to Keats.

Finally: A lesser poet might have taken this subject as an occasion to virtue-signal about the malignant alien aridity of anyone knowing or wanting to know anything about atoms and particles and such. But here are this last poem's last words:

> And in this probing: what I close
> my hand on, name, forget. Then want again.

The word for this is curiosity, a necessary compulsion repeatedly exercised—quickened and repaid—in, for instance, the grasping/ ungrasping minds of an experimental scientist, of a certain extraordinary kind of poet, and of the reader of these extraordinary poems.

SHE WOULD HAVE LIKED THIS

James Cervantes

Just a few nights ago, before I started writing this, I had a dream. In that dream, I was perusing a very odd book of different sizes and thickness of pages in various colors. Wendy was looking over my left shoulder. Some pages had printed text, poetry and prose, others just a footnote or a link to something on the internet, and a few blossomed into paintings or drawings larger than the page that had given them birth. Some became a film. How would I reference these pages, I wondered aloud, since I would have to teach from the book. I turned to Wendy and she said, "It doesn't matter."

Dream became conscious thought and I realized dream-Wendy had given me the freedom to write of once-corporeal Wendy and her poetry in a way that mirrors the poetry and her virtual interactions with the world in her final years. As in many writer/friend relationships these days, I met Wendy via the internet and a listserv on which we and other poets and writers interacted. Wendy and I soon discovered we had many things in common: both lucid dreamers, with interests in anthropology and archeology, in which we'd both taken courses at the University of Washington while in the writing program there, though at different times. And, of course, the virtual world of the internet and its role as medium and technique in poetry and other writings, as well as in teaching.

Enter Facebook, where poetry, dreams, and diary merge and become a sort of enhanced haibun in which poets and dreamers can splash happily. Wendy took to it easily, though clouds appeared early on. In exploring her Facebook timeline, I came across an entry for December 10th, 2012:

> Woke this morning with a dream image: a calendar of December that had an X through today and was blank thereafter. No days remaining. Should wake that way every day.

I flashed forward and backward to 2014. I was busy selecting, soliciting, and editing poetry for the forthcoming anthology *In Like Company*, and urged Wendy to gather several recent short poems under the title "Elementals." The final section read:

> The last question and then
> the test is over. What will you do
> when you're dead? Knit,
> if you don't. There's no end to knitting.
> Go on speaking into the silence
> as if it were keepsake.
> Take care of the cat,
> the cat is still alive, and so
> too a man, no rest
> when the world ends.

And I think of Fu, her cat, still alive, and Wendy dead, alone.

Dream. Life. Poetry. October 7, 2015:

> Legacy is an accident that happens to someone else. When I was sick in the hospital some time ago, a helpful person had my place cleaned. I came home to find my desk dismantled, my papers, books, and work dumped into tall immovable heavy

boxes. This, after a lifetime of saying "Just don't touch the desk."
Perhaps I've been in shock for months. I'm just beginning
to accept that I might never find my current journal, my pocket
Moleskin, the binder of poems for this book. I keep fat journals,
the kind that slip into a leather cover while in service and sit
labeled on a shelf once the next volume starts. This one was
almost full. **But who, with the waters rising, will bother to
rescue one more life's work when I'm gone? Foolish to make
a life of words.**

"Elementals" was to be one of Wendy Battin's last publications. It
appeared in *In Like Company: The Porch & Salt River Review Anthology*,
April, 2015, MadHat Press. The penultimate section of "Elementals":

> You can wipe the memory
> from your phone, as if you'd never spoken.
> Wipe your hard drive. Burn your poems.
> Some government remembers
> but you aren't a person of interest
> or not so much. **The word is still
> in the river, caught
> in the tide pools but cut
> loose when the water rises.**

I have put some of those words in bold to point out what I saw and
felt happening in the poetry, the life, and daily musings. It had begun
earlier:

September 11, 2015: Everything near has drifted away.

September 30, 2015: Inside, cough and fever. Outside,
rain's / fingertips, rain's knuckles.

Then, on November 2, 2015, Wendy posted this poem, one in which
she is engaged with death in a larger context and we see again a spark
of the delightful word play and humor of which she was master.

And, fittingly, the poem was a ghostly reiteration of a posting from November 2, 2014:

Day of the Dead

The underworld, earth, and heaven, three
shelves of the altar. The middle world

on the middle shelf, how the gaze dwells
right in the center, the living who are dead to us

however we love them. Breathe copal, the resin
of amber, the preserver. I will be that dragonfly

perfect in your hand, a golden gem
held up to the light

anonymous in your pocket. The first shelf
all inheritance, a harrowing of what's not hell

but being born. In heaven as it deserves to be
Galway, Seamus, Flannery,

a crowded solitary party
where all have their Underwoods.

I read that on the screen here in San Miguel de Allende, where I and others would go that night to parade with the living dressed as the dead.

Then, on December 2, 2015, she posted, quite simply: I hear a mouse.

The hair on my neck went up.

*— James Cervantes, October 1, 2019,
San Miguel de Allende*

A PILLAR OF WATER

Alfred Corn

At a certain point in a writer's career, authors (many of them friends or professional acquaintances) send their books to you in large numbers, books that occupy much of the time you have for reading. So you have trouble getting to new books that are *not* sent, all the more in that you have to go to a bookstore to seek them out. I had heard of Wendy Battin for many years, but we hadn't met; and, since neither of her two books arrived in the mail, I hadn't read her work. The first meeting came after Leslie McGrath's book launch in October of 2009 at a bookstore in Mystic. There followed a little party at the James Merrill House in Stonington, a house where, many years earlier, I'd been a constant guest of Merrill's—in fact, I'd spent two summers in that house when he was away in Greece. In the intervening years, after the house had been transformed into a residence for visiting writers, many of the artworks Merrill owned and some of the familiar furniture had been removed. The place looked sort of bare to me, and I was feeling a little low-spirited, predictably focusing on impermanence, loss, etc., as I sat on the sofa in the upstairs space where Merrill used to entertain. A woman short in stature and with a curly mop of hair came and sat beside me, introducing herself as Wendy Battin. We spoke pleasantly for a while, her ironic humor a good antidote to the mood I was in. By the end of the party, we'd exchanged telephone numbers, which led to a meeting the following month. She drove up to Rhode Island for coffee and cake, an hour during which we got to know each other amazingly well. It was the beginning of a warm friendship, with visits back and forth between Rhode Island and Mystic. I remember we shared a Thanksgiving dinner at my place, just she and I, neither of us much involved with family connections. Also, as well I could tell, Wendy had no active friendships in Mystic apart from regular contact with Charles Hartman—reunions frequent and warm, even though they no longer lived together. That friendship, and the company of her beloved cat Fu, seemed to be enough for her. It's a little surprising that she added me to a very small circle she made little effort to expand.

I began reading her first book (titled *In the Solar Wind*), immediately impressed by her fluency and originality. It wasn't easy to "place" her work in the Balkanized territory of contemporary poetry. But she had spoken several times admiringly of Seamus Heaney, and of William Matthews, whom she knew at Cornell, and who later recruited her for the graduate program at the University of Washington. He chose her first book as one of the winners in the National Poetry Series for 1984. She also spoke affectionately of Merrill, whom she referred to by his first name. The authors you admire say a lot about you, so I began to think of Wendy as one of those poets productively concerned, not with content solely, but with verbal expression. For such poets, feeling develops in the background rather than up front in the glare of footlights. She wasn't sentimental, but instead acute and precise, the poems powered by an emotion reined in rather than shouted from the rooftops. There was always something elusive in her poems, leaving room for speculation; you couldn't sum up their meanings in a pat phrase.

I gradually became aware that Wendy drank too much, something I discussed with Leslie McGrath, who knew Wendy, though they were not close. Myself, I came of age at a time when most writers drank unapologetically, so Wendy's propensities in that direction didn't surprise me at all. Yet I had difficulty squaring it away with her yoga practice (she taught yoga at the local Y), which was very, very important to her. She had falls more than once, the injuries from them (until she healed) sabotaging direct demonstration of the poses for her students. Eventually, I recommended AA meetings, and she did attend a couple of times but didn't feel at home in the small-town, religiose atmosphere of Mystic's AA community. I'm pretty sure she'd have made a go of it if she'd lived in Boston or New York, where she would have met people more like herself. The result was that she began to decline and eventually lost her job at the Y. When that happened, I was afraid that being by herself all day with no external responsibilities would propel her still further down, and those fears were realized. I'd rather not speak in detail about her last year, when Charles Hartman, Leslie McGrath and I did what we could to help Wendy, in the face of very serious illness, with no readily available solution.

When I think of this friend, I recall her keen, ironic intelligence; her ardent feminism; her pride in being Irish-American; her great respect for natural science; her contempt for religion and its repressions, particularly those forced on women. There was also a certain disdain she felt for poets who were not the real article, those whose lack of excellence nevertheless hadn't stood in the way of their becoming stars on the poetry scene. Believe me, we had many a good laugh about glaring absurdities in the pobiz world.

She, however, was the real thing. Crisp diction, economy, fine-tuned imagery, wide reading, and a flair for unusual subjects: those are her earmarks. Yet thoughtfulness and refinement can, unfortunately, constitute a barrier to popularity; the audience normally prefers something more sensational. I don't know all of Wendy's life story, so I can't say if the very long interval between her first and second books was the result of choice or merely the typical up-and-down oscillation of a career that couldn't count on many external supports. It doesn't matter. *Little Apocalypse* marks a notable gain in range and expression over the first book.

Not incidentally, it contains the shattering "The Women on the Ward," which, along with the book's title, might count as a hint that clouds were gathering.

I don't like to use the word "tragic" loosely, but the word almost does describe Wendy's too-short lifespan, during which she overcame some, but only some, of the hindrances connected to her disadvantaged childhood, her gender, and inevitable shifts in personal relationships. In the face of many negatives, it's a consolation to see that her work is being reissued, giving the readership an opportunity to discover or rediscover it. Spending time with Wendy's poetry as I prepared these comments has been a strong pleasure, which, because I knew her personally, involves a wide spectrum of associations, some painful, some exhilarating. It's always inaccurate to name just one poem as the epitome of a life and a work, but, if forced to, I would mention "Christine Falls on the Road to Paradise," which was published as the opening poem in Wendy's first book. It struck a note, one that continued to echo in various guises throughout a notably distinguished body of work. Wendy Battin was a source, and that pillar of water continues to flow.

—Alfred Corn, March 2019,
Rhode Island.

In all This noise the self makes
the rash of static in the body
the nerves firing like snipers
in the panics of memory
the slide
into drug stupor or drug transparency
in which everything is light except
the self, which is merely
~~the self~~ a tourist —

in the anxiety of love, which is always
an emptying into space
from which nothing comes back —

there is no ~~comfort~~ for
a body out of love with itself

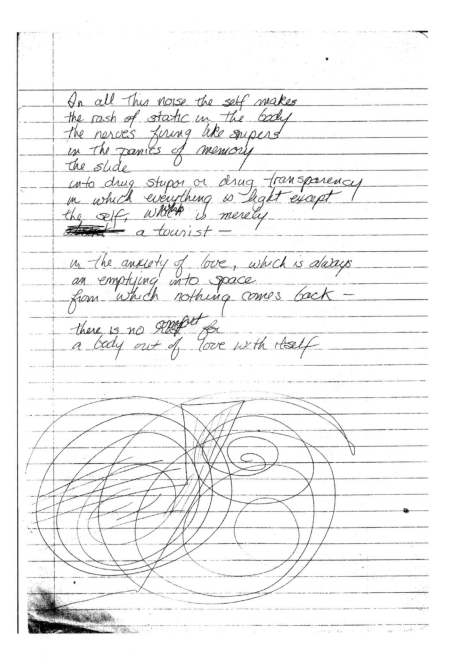

Make them quiet, the crowd tasks:
in the wings; ~~we~~ we have ~~something~~
that require silence. Set the dog
to watch them, and
set the lion to watch the dog,
lest he bark. If thunder and rain
break the quiet we'll make it
part of our work. ~~When~~ the cat howls
it drives away demons. All this
we will make our new silence, our screen
for the shadow play.

                    The ~~birds~~ crows split air with their ~~song~~ caw.
                    Make them silent. The fan hums;
                    it's ~~a~~ summer ~~day~~ thick as

~~The crows the birds~~

                                    Hush
The crows wax discordant. ~~Silence them~~.
This day in July is thick as a ~~pond~~ cowpond
with algae. The fan hums its rising
~~still~~ and falling tune. Make it still.
The crowd in the ~~street,~~ escaping
from attics. ~~and~~ It is hot. Yes it's hot.
Make them quiet.

We have tasks that require
silence.

The computer returns us to perspective & to 2 dimensions

trace

'The lab fills with the paraphernalia of
engineers: a spectrgraph, fee the division
of light,the pressurized tanks, the oscilloscope,
with its screee resolving thecurrent in
waves, stopped into trails of repetitious like
Egyptian heiroglyphics no like Egyptian relief;
the terminal will not answer unless addressed
with perfect etiquette, a diplomatic tongue,
it can be told Fatal Hardware Error; it cannot
be told I'M DYING SEND FOR THE POLICE THIS IS
MY BORTHDAY ILOVEYOU THIS MEANS THAT I'M WATCHING
MY LIFE FLOW OUT OF ME LIKE PHOTONS.
there is a chamber where ~~a mechanized/mechanical butterfly~~ sheetmetal butterfly is flapping its
ponderous wings.Slow as an eagle's, slow as a x
a ~~electrical~~ sign ~~in a steady~~ in a persistent
wind. ~~A methodogy of flight, no~~ a methodolgy
of wavering, ~~a physics of wavering~~, a physics
of suspension.

It is a window through which we see the current.

resolving the current into a trace of light:
across acidic green screeen, the trace
strung on a grid resolved into the relief on the
tomb's rock wall: this means that m my days ①
repeat and repeat, that what passes for change
in the readings is statistical, that there is
only a standard variation from day to day. ②
What I do must be repeated elsewhere,
reproduced under similar conditions in
the next state, the opposite/apposite country.
But we are like bees. There is nowhere we can't
be found:intercom, beam phone, public address. ③
In every way we can be reached. We can always
be reached. The lab fills with the paraphernalia
of talk.

a glass house, or one glass room in a ~~house~~ of mirrors.

The butterfly flaps its sheet-metal ponderous w
wings. It seems that the air comes off the ~~to~~
surfaces like smoke rings, in tiny puffs; ④
what holds the thing aloft; A fruit fly drosophila
on the other hand rows with its wings--they
meet abovve & below the fly, vaguely, at this
speed, so slow that the Mylar/plastic turns as
a leaf does toward sun. This is an enginee~~ring~~
problem we are solving; this is a technical
problem

*tomb-
Egyptian
relief*

stop

*now start - new building
an atom bomb
on an ant
~~farm~~*

bees again

1.. When she was little, she played with toy dinosaurs, wrote plays
and tried to recruit the neighborhood children to act them, wrote
a neighborhood newspaper and peddled it door to door. She was
taken to mass on sundays, after battling her mother each morning
over unwanted dreasses, scratchy crinolines, the painful brush
through her long hair. She flew once, off a swing at its highest
arc, forward across the yard to a flat gray stone; rose; walked
to the back steps; fell again. Her mother watched from the
kitchen door, convinced she was dead, and would not go out to her.
When she started school, she insisted on walking the one block
alone. She read a picture encyclopedia:Maya, mathematics, aviation,
astronomy. She made a colored clay world for the gray brontosaurus,
the blue Tyrannosaur, a cliff for the red pteranodon, and took
it to the nun.She was homely and too good a student, and the children
sent her home often in tears. The tears came easily, and she did
not know it was possible to stop them. She gave things away. She
told what she thought was the truth, and never understood why
they called her a liar. Her mother stood her on the double bed
and made her swear, on the dark wood crucifix, on the deepening
bronze gaunt Christ, that she would not lie; the world spun, and
she was terrified, because she could not swear to what she could
not understand---not with her hand on the terriblemetallic body,
which hung over the bed where her parents slept. She refused to
admit she was a girl, that she would be a woman, for she saw what
it would mean: a small life, in dresses, the body forbidden to
move, the feet always on tiptoe, propped by thin spikes. Neither
Maya nor mathematics, neither dinosaurs nor aviation, neither before
man nor past him, but always waiting for him in the present,
waiting for his approval which never came. She thought she would
avert it with a word: no. No, I am not, not this, not that.

Διόνυσος παῖ Τίγρις (ΔΗΛΟΣ)

Dionysis and Tiger: Mosaic at Delos

The god has the full red lips of a woman, and wings
~~and~~
~~and~~
unfurled over his golden shoulders. The intricate netting
of feathers frames him.
~~He~~ is pouting and ~~fretful~~. The dark grout
~~the~~ rimming the chips of tile
read as shadow, depth to the eyesockets, ~~the~~
aging ~~pores~~ to the skin, immortal but
dissolute.
Where the torso should be, ~~bare~~ plaster:
~~into~~ irregular seacoast:
~~into~~ the god-marked land the water spreads
But the eyes: the eyes are watchful, cast
~~toward the great~~ tiger's great head.
The tiger also disembodied, though here the mosaic
is whole. ~~Her~~ massive carnivorous head
rises out of a bed of what must have been flowers,
foliage, tiger at wood's edge, and here
the bleached tiles vein each leaf with light,
as if the sun locked in their cells could shine.
The tiger is prayerful, her eyes raised ~~up,~~
her tongue comes forth to speak,
as any cat looks ~~prayerful~~ watching
a bird ~~to light to~~ above,
~~its~~ unreachable flashing wings.
Her green eyes ~~are~~ are human, rimmed with
white. ~~as any woman would here~~,

And what was lost ~~in~~ to time, where the mosaic
falls away.
from here, the plaster chipped edges
~~spreads from~~

Irregular as seacoast
→ featurelesswater spreads
on the god-marked land

draw back
& see at
map at
end?

Mondrian

b. 1872, March 7

first learned to paint 1880, aged 8
studied in Amsterdam 5 years (20-25)

aged 30 in 1902
First exhibition 1909 (36)

Quoted exactly:
1912. Influenced by Cubist painting. Changes his name
from Mondriaan to Mondrian.
—(Mondrian, Italo Tomassoni; Hamlyn Ped.
NY 1970)

1913 — first abstract works (@41) !
in Paris 1911-1914, 1919-1938; London 1938-40; NYC 1940-44
30's 1902 -1912
40's 1912 — 1922   1916 meets Theosophist
50's 1922-32
60's 1932-42
d. 1944, before his 72nd birthday

Mondrian is a Mandala-maker — yantra?
but he tends toward the ~~three~~fold level of structure,
the 3 dimensional + physically ~~~~ expansive, rather than
to the one-pointedness of circular mandala, or of
the Oval Compositions.

The subconscious is still very off active in the earlier
abstractions, as in Oval Composition 1913; human
faces and bodies appear; in abstracted expression of emotion
and create narrative content.

The gradual "depopulation" of the paintings, the
"pure geometry," ~~~~ brings him to an alternate
consciousness, contemplation of rhythm + structure
(essentially the same thing). Would he have returned
to the human world eventually, with that skill mastered?
(bodhisattva?)

To what extent was his project "reductive"?

The "end" of the food chain: the gods who eat
the thoughts of men (who are in turn
eaten by the universe, the Atman, and
give back the energy to keep ~~the~~ the Dance
going?)

Dear D:

Lately when I look ~~for a dream~~ rifle my catalogue
of dreams, looking for comfort
looking for somewhere to rest alive
in, all my landscapes elude me.
The ~~beach~~ I imagine is ~~as sullen~~
as my room,

but ~~forgetting~~ deserting the landscape
I can love the sea. I think
especially of the whales
passing their songs around the globe,
and all the ocean is a mind
with a tune running through it,
over and over, heard before
breakfast and impossible to shake.

One
One has married her solitude,
    wants a divorce.
One imagines that she
    has not been understood.
One imagines she has.

The pages collect on my desk, interleaved
like hands joined, swearing a public oath.
What are we swearing to? We are
nearing from state to state,
    as they say of excited electrons, or
of water as it freezes
and sublimes,
or of the mind when it enters a drug
like an airplane.
It rocked at Maria's wharf for months,
waiting for cranes from New Bedford to lift it
bodily, as we all wait.

In another room now, or
another ocean.

Far Good
The Prayer Flags

Poem as green sky and tornadoes and flying lapdogs.
Poem as the powerPoem as the Pekinese monsoon?
Poem as bicycle broken in half, so two may ride unicycles. lines waiting to be blown down again.
Poem that Daisy is waiting to finish. Poem without end.
and as he is mouser and softly sure-footed. As we are mice.
poem of leaving our bodies and linking our minds, poem of the hive.
poem of the solitaire, cut for the light.
poem of freeing the cat from the fence, poem as flash flood, when javelinas run through the house near-sighted snout to butt.

The poem of our hoarding from death what death doesn't want.

Glass shouldn't cry out? The sand of its trials is the beach you walk on.

By the world in its mud and blues I am so renewed that even the words glow, each a firefly in my hand, clapping its wings in green code.

it creates a world in a bottle in the heart of the artist. It works in tandem like Vishnu and Shiva to bring that world alive and keep it so. It ends and begins again.

Three birds, a cardinal and two sparrows on the wires. Cat watches them through a screen. I watch the birds through the cat and I watch the birds.
Listen.

CONTRIBUTORS' & EDITORS' NOTES

CONTRIBUTORS' NOTES

SHARON BRYAN is the author of four books of poems, most recently *Sharp Stars* from BOA. She is also the editor of *Where We Stand: Women Poets on Literary Tradition*, and co-editor, with William Olsen, of *Planet on the Table: Poets on the Reading Life*. She teaches in the Lesley University Low-Residency MFA Program in Cambridge, Massachusetts.

JAMES CERVANTES has published six books of poetry, most recently *Sleepwalker's Songs: New & Selected Poems*. He is the editor of *In Like Company: The Porch & Salt River Review Anthology*, published by MadHat Press. Cervantes has been publishing poetry in print since 1969 and almost exclusively online since 1997.

ALFRED CORN has published eleven books of poems, the most recent titled *Unions*, and two novels, the second titled *Miranda's Book*. Of his three collections of essays, the most recent is titled *Arks & Covenants*. He has received the Guggenheim, the NEA, an Award in Literature from the Academy of Arts and Letters, and one from the Academy of American Poets.

JOHN GORDON is Professor Emeritus of English at Connecticut College. He is a graduate of Hamilton College and has a doctorate from Harvard University. He is the author of six books, three of them on James Joyce. He is currently working on an internet site entitled *John Gordon's Finnegans Wake Blog*.

JULIE KANE is a former National Poetry Series winner, Fulbright Scholar, and Louisiana Poet Laureate. With Grace Bauer, she co-edited *Nasty Women Poets: An Unapologetic Anthology of Subversive Verse* (Lost Horse Press, 2017). Her most recent book of poems is *Mothers of Ireland* (LSU Press, 2020).

STEPHEN TAPSCOTT is a poet who lives and works in Cambridge, Massachusetts. He is the translator, most recently, of *Georg Trakl: Poems*, in the Field Translation Series.

EDITORS' NOTES

PAMELA ALEXANDER is the author of four collections of poems, including *Slow Fire* (Ausable/Copper Canyon, 2007). Earlier books won the Yale Younger Poet and Iowa Poetry awards, and her work has appeared in numerous anthologies and journals. She taught creative writing at M.I.T. and Oberlin College for many years.

MARTHA COLLINS has published ten books of poetry, most recently *Because What Else Could I Do* (Pittsburgh, 2019). She has also published four co-translated volumes of Vietnamese poetry and co-edited several anthologies, including (with Kevin Prufer), *Into English: Poems, Translations, Essays* (Graywolf, 2017). She founded the creative writing program at U. Mass-Boston and taught creative writing at Oberlin College for ten years.

CHARLES HARTMAN has published seven books of poetry, including *New & Selected Poems* (Ahsahta, 2008), as well as books on jazz and song (*Jazz Text*) and on computer poetry (*Virtual Muse*). His *Free Verse: An Essay on Prosody* (1981) is still in print, and *Verse: An Introduction to Prosody* came out from Wiley-Blackwell in 2015. He is Poet in Residence at Connecticut College. He plays jazz guitar.

MATTHEW KRAJNIAK is an Inprint C. Glenn Cambor Fellow of Literature and Creative Writing at the University of Houston. His interviews and fiction have most recently appeared in *Gulf Coast, Poetry Foundation*, and *The Avalon Literary Review*.

ACKNOWLEDGMENTS

The editors are immensely grateful to the Unsung Masters Series Board for making this book possible. We would also like to thank Niki Herd, who lent her experience and wisdom; Julie Kane, who preserved, located, and gave us access to Wendy Battin's early poems; and Ashley Hanson and Andrew Lopez, Research Librarians at Connecticut College.

We are also grateful to the editors of presses and periodicals where Wendy Battin's work first or most recently appeared:

The Ashland Poetry Press: *Little Apocalypse* (Ashland, Ohio, 1997). Thanks to the Press for permission to reprint poems from that volume.

Doubleday: *In the Solar Wind* (New York, 1984)

The following publications, where some of the late poems first appeared:

Cimarron Review: "Four Poems" (Fall 2015)

FIELD: "The Ferry Lies Down on a Sharp Rock" and "An Asterisk Named Fred Astaire" (Spring 2001)

Hamilton Stone Review: "Mercy 1" and "Mir, the World, or is it Peace,"(Fall 2003)

In Like Company, ed. James Cervantes: "Elementals" (MadHat, 2015)

Salt River Review: "Liberty" (Winter 2001-2)

Visions, Voices, and Verses: Anthology for the New Britain Museum of American Art, ed. Colin Haskins and Andrea Barton: "Clown with Drum" (Exiles Press, 2012)

The following publications, where some of the early poems first appeared:

Chiaroscuro: "October: A Love Poem" and "In the Forest She
    Thinks of the Greater Body" (1976)
The First Anthology, ed. A. R. Ammons et al: "Letter Toward a
    Successful Escape" (1975)
Granite: "On Hearing of Suicides, and the Value of Chanting"
    and "She Awaits His Wrath" (Winter 1976-77)
Mademoiselle: "The Revolution" (March 1978) [Editors' note:
    Wendy Battin won an Honorable Mention in
    Mademoiselle's 1975 College Poetry Competition.]
The Stone: "The Time Warp" and "Scat on the Observable
    Universe" (1975)

This book is produced as a collaboration among
Gulf Coast: A Journal of Literature and Fine Art
and
Copper Nickel
and
Pleiades: Literature in Context

GENEROUS SUPPORT AND FUNDING PROVIDED BY:

The Nancy Luton Fund
Cynthia Woods Mitchell Center for the Arts
Houston Arts Alliance
University of Houston
Missouri Arts Council
University of Central Missouri
National Endowment for the Arts

This book is set in Adobe Caslon Pro type
with Ostrich Sans Inline and Dense titles.

Designed and typeset by Martin Rock.